Small Plates for Sharing

Pictured on front cover: Tostada Cups with Lemony Lentils and Spinach, page 18
Pictured on right: Cappuccino Meringue Stack, page 146

Nutrition Information Guidelines

Each recipe has been analysed using the Canadian Nutrient File from Health Canada, which is based upon the United States Department of Agriculture (USDA) Nutrient Database.
- If more than one ingredient is listed (such as 'hard margarine or butter'), or if a range is given (5–10 mL, 1–2 tsp.), only the first ingredient or first amount is analysed.
- The lesser number of servings is used if a range is stated.
- Ingredients indicating 'sprinkle', 'optional' or 'for garnish' are not included in the nutrition information.
- Milk used is 1% M.F. (milk fat), unless otherwise noted.

Vera Mazurak, Ph.D (Nutritionist)

We gratefully acknowledge the following suppliers for their generous support of our test and photo kitchens:

Broil King Barbecues	Hamilton Beach® Canada	Proctor Silex® Canada
Corelle®	Lagostina®	Tupperware®

Our special thanks to the following businesses for providing numerous props for photography:

Stokes	Mikasa Home Store	Danesco Inc.
Winners Stores	Emile Henry	Wal-Mart Canada Inc.
The Bay	Canhome Global	Klass Works
Pier 1 Imports®	Totally Bamboo	Out of the Fire Studio
Cherison Enterprises Inc.		

Small Plates for Sharing
Copyright © Company's Coming Publishing Limited

Published in 2010 by Hinkler Books Pty Ltd
45–55 Fairchild Street
Heatherton
Victoria 3202 Australia
www.hinklerbooks.com

10 9 8 7 6 5 4 3 2
15 14 13 12 11

ISBN: 978 1 7418 5401 5

Printed and bound in China

Originally published by
Company's Coming Publishing Limited
2311 – 96 Street
Edmonton, Alberta, Canada T6N 1G3
Tel: 780-450-6223   Fax: 780-450-1857
www.companyscoming.com

Company's Coming is a registered trademark owned by Company's Coming Publishing Limited

Contents

The Company's Coming Legacy   6
Foreword   7
Cocktails   8

Beds & Pillows   10
Piquant nibbles cradled by vegetables, bread or pastry

• Roasted Spinach Portobellos • Spiced Jam with Heady Garlic and Cambozola • Creamy Wild Mushrooms on Pastry Points • Tostada Cups with Lemony Lentils and Spinach • Potato Crostini with Caramelised Bacon • Five-spiced Crepes with Coconut Scallops • Pear Puff Tart • Seafood with Horseradish Beetroot Coulis • Grecian Beef Pastries

Little Bowls   30
Heady dips, hot and cold soups, rich risottos and succulent mélanges

• Panini Sticks with Dipping Trio • Seafood Bisque • Sun-dried Tomato and Leek Mussels • Smoked Salmon Blintz Cups • Mango Gazpacho • Coconut Chilli Soup • Miso Mushroom Risotto with Scallops • Butter Chicken with Spinach and Pappadums

Maverick Morsels   48
Inspired twists on favourite flavours

• Seared Beef Carpaccio with Peppercorn Mushrooms • Peanut Noodle Cakes with Sweet Chilli Seafood • 'Uptown' Goat Cheese Potato Skins • Sweet Polenta Fries with Jalapeño Lime Dip • Walnut Pesto-crusted Lamb with Cranberry Port Jus • Margarita Chicken Lollipops • Crab Sushi Squares • Savoury Shortbread Trio • Fiery Plantain Chips with Cocomango Dip • Walnut Ginger Crisps • Halibut Bites in Peppered Panko Crust • Prawn Corn Cakes with Lime Sauce

On The Green   74
Glorious ways with leafy and vegetable greens

• Almond Brie Croutons on Apple-dressed Spinach • Smoked Tuna and Wasabi Cream in Endive Boats • Seared Scallops Verde • Warm Ginger Chicken over Spinach • Praline Pecans, Beetroot and Blue Cheese on Baby Greens • Miso-glazed Cod on Ginger-spiked Cucumbers • Salmon with Herb Sabayon • Chilli Squid on Garlic Peas • Herb Olive Feta Mélange over Grilled Asparagus • Caramel Pork Tenderloin on Bok Choy

Rolled Up & Tucked In — 96
Tenderly wrapped or filled temptations

• Feta and Herb Eggplant (Aubergine) Rolls • Curried Chicken Samosa Strudel • Seafood Mango Summer Rolls with Cool Herbs and Chilli Heat • Rocket Pesto Ravioli with Browned Butter Pine Nuts • Mushroom Risotto Balls • Crispy Jerk Chicken Rolls • Parmesan Cones with Cannellini Mousse • Seta Antojitos Especial • Smoked Salmon Rice Rolls

Skewered — 116
Clever queues of delectable bites

• Dukkah Beef Skewers with Wine Reduction • Chicken Saltimbocca Spikes • Thai Chicken on Lemongrass Skewers • Leek-wrapped Ginger Scallops with Soy Glaze • Rosemary-spiked Meatballs • Mahogany Chicken Waves • Chilli-crusted Medallions • Sesame Chilli Vegetable Skewers • Tuna Skewers • Pork Souvlaki with Savoury Yoghurt • Candied Chicken Sticks

Small & Sweet — 140
Petite yet powerful dessert temptations

• Halvah Ice-cream Sundaes with Orange Honey Figs • Crisp Cinnamon Banana Boats • Cappuccino Meringue Stack • Raspberry Crème Brûlée • Caramel Rum S'Mores • Lavalicious Chocolate Kisses • Pomegranate Jellies • Ginger-poached Pears • Vanillacotta with Liqueur

Simply Sophisticated — 160
Ordinary foods dressed to the nines

• Lemon Thyme Sorbet • Calabrese Bites • Braised Hoisin Spareribs • Prosciutto-wrapped Bread Sticks with Cantaloupe Purée • Strawberry Salsa with Goat Cheese and Melba Toast • Jalapeño Corn Soup • Coconut Lime Chicken Salad Cocktails • Tapenade Toasts • Nut, Cheese and Fruit Bites • Salty-sweet Croustades

Glossary	182
Menu Suggestions	184
Tip Index	185
Recipe Index	186
Measurement Tables	191

The Company's Coming Legacy

Jean Paré grew up with an understanding that family, friends and home cooking are the key ingredients for a good life. A busy mother of four, Jean developed a knack for creating quick and easy recipes using everyday ingredients. For 18 years, she operated a successful catering business from her home kitchen in the small prairie town of Vermilion, Alberta, Canada. During that time, she earned a reputation for great food, courteous service and reasonable prices. Steadily increasing demand for her recipes led to the founding of Company's Coming Publishing Limited in 1981.

The first Company's Coming cookbook, *150 Delicious Squares*, was an immediate bestseller. As more titles were introduced, the company quickly earned the distinction of publishing Canada's most popular cookbooks. Company's Coming continues to gain new supporters in Canada, the United States and throughout the world by adhering to Jean's Golden Rule of Cooking: *never share a recipe you wouldn't use yourself*. It's an approach that has worked – millions of times over!

A familiar and trusted name in the kitchen, Company's Coming has extended its reach throughout the home with other types of books and products for everyday living.

Though humble about her achievements, Jean Paré is one of North America's most loved and recognised authors. The recipient of many awards, Jean was appointed Member of the Order of Canada, her country's highest lifetime achievement honour.

Today, Jean Paré's influence as founding author, mentor and moral compass is evident in all aspects of the company she founded. Every recipe created and every product produced upholds the family values and work ethic she instilled. Readers the world over will continue to be encouraged and inspired by her legacy for generations to come.

Foreword

Good company and great food create a powerful combination. When laughter and conversation mix with the heady fragrance and flavours of delicious fare, we are not just sharing a meal – we are nourishing our lives. Artfully prepared dishes awaken the senses and please the palate. And here's the secret: it can all be so simple!

This title features full-page colour photos of every recipe, menu suggestions, sidebars on preparation tips and tricks, how-to photos, imaginative presentation ideas and helpful entertaining information to allow you and your guests to really savour the food – and your time together. The focus is on smaller portions – think tapas, hors d'oeuvres or antipasti. Novice cooks and experienced chefs will value the range of flavours, ethnic influences, gorgeous photographs and step-by-step instructions.

The French have a name for a small bite with big impact – *amuse bouche* – literally, something that amuses the mouth. In the following eight chapters, great care and attention have been given to combinations of flavour, texture and presentation so that you and your guests can explore great food possibilities, one delicious mouthful after another.

Guests will appreciate your thoughtfulness and skill, while you revel in how easy it was to prepare these impressive morsels. *Small Plates for Sharing* lets you cook and entertain in a relaxed atmosphere – and have fun doing so.

Approachable recipes, fabulous results, wonderful get-togethers – it all starts with *Small Plates for Sharing*.

Atmosphere. A fantastic cocktail gets your guests in the mood for socialising and sets the tone for the evening. Whether it be a simple, classic martini or an elaborate and colourful cocktail, this will be the first taste your guests enjoy. Here are a few favourites to try, each with a modern twist on tradition.

Cocktails

Blue Lagoon

Pour 1 part white (light) rum, 1/2 part lychee liqueur and 2 parts orange juice over ice in a chilled cocktail glass. Add 5 mL (1 tsp.) lemon juice and top with soda water. Drizzle with 1 part blue-coloured, bitter orange liqueur and allow it to settle to the bottom.

Bueno Beer Margaritas

In a pitcher, combine a 340 mL (12 oz.) lime juice cordial with equal parts water, beer and tequila. Add 60 mL (1/4 cup) orange liqueur. Serve over crushed ice in margarita glasses.

Canadian Snowbird

Pour 1 part Canadian whiskey (rye), 4 parts apple juice and 1/2 part each of peach schnapps, lemon liqueur and maple syrup over ice in a chilled cocktail glass. Squeeze a lemon wedge over top and drop in.

Mojitos

Using a wooden spoon, crush or 'muddle' 3 cut-up limes with 40 mint leaves and 60 mL (1/4 cup) sugar in a 1 litre (1 qt) pitcher. Add 60 mL (1/4 cup) lime cordial, if desired, to make a sweeter cocktail. Stir in 170 mL (6 oz.) rum and add ice until pitcher is 3/4 full. Top with soda water. Serve in cocktail glasses.

Orange Truffletini

Combine 1 part vanilla vodka, 1 part chocolate liqueur and 1/2 part orange liqueur in a martini glass.

Piña Colada Martini

Combine 1 part coconut rum, 3/4 part orange vodka and 2 parts pineapple juice with crushed ice in a cocktail shaker. Shake and strain into a cocktail glass. Drop in a cherry and add a drizzle of grenadine.

Pomcosmo

Combine 2 parts lemon vodka, 2 parts pomegranate juice and 1 part orange liqueur with crushed ice in a cocktail shaker. Shake and strain into a cocktail glass.

Inviting. The allure of these morsels may put you in mind of sweet dreams, but their flavours will enliven your senses. Discover savoury delights nestled on canapé beds of bread, pastry – even mushroom caps, beetroot coulis or potato crostini. Like Goldilocks before you, you can experiment:
which bed and which pillow are just right for you?

Beds & Pillows

Piquant nibbles cradled by vegetables, bread or pastry

Roasted Spinach Portobellos

Ingredient	Metric	Imperial
Large portobello mushrooms, gills removed (see Tip, below)	2	2
Butter-flavoured cooking spray		
Bacon slices, diced	2	2
Chopped fresh spinach leaves, lightly packed	500 mL	2 cups
Basil pesto	50 mL	3 tbsp.
Fine dry breadcrumbs	30 mL	2 tbsp.
Grated Italian cheese blend (or a mixture of Parmesan, Cheddar and Mozzarella cheeses)	175 mL	3/4 cup
Pine nuts	10 mL	2 tsp.
Prepared tomato pasta sauce	60 mL	1/4 cup

Remove and chop mushroom stems. Set aside. Spray both sides of mushroom caps with cooking spray and place, stem-side down, on a baking tray. Bake in a 190°C (375°F) oven for 10 minutes.

Cook bacon in a frying pan until crisp. Add mushroom stems and cook for about 5 minutes until softened and liquid is evaporated.

Stir in spinach leaves and pesto and cook until spinach is softened. Remove from heat.

Stir in breadcrumbs and half of cheese. Spoon into mushroom caps. Sprinkle with remaining cheese and pine nuts. Bake for 10 to 15 minutes until heated through and golden. Cut into quarters.

Swirl some tomato sauce on a serving plate. Arrange mushroom wedges over sauce, drizzling remaining sauce over top. Makes 8 wedges.

1 wedge: 515 Kilojoules (123 Calories); 9.0 g Total Fat (1.4 g Mono, 0.6 g Poly, 3.1 g Sat); 13 mg Cholesterol; 5 g Carbohydrate; 1 g Fibre; 6 g Protein; 216 mg Sodium

GARNISH
Sprig of fresh basil

TIP
Because the gills can sometimes be bitter, be sure to remove them from the portobellos before stuffing. First remove the stems, then, using a small spoon, scrape out and discard the mushroom gills.

EXPERIMENT!
Use a prepared bruschetta mix in place of tomato sauce for a different taste and texture.

Stuffed mushrooms are always a crowd-pleaser. Using large portobellos in place of smaller mushrooms makes for a unique presentation and easier prep. Pairs perfectly with other Italian-flavoured small plates.

Spiced Jam
with Heady Garlic and Cambozola

Ingredient	Metric	Imperial
Olive oil	5 mL	1 tsp.
Chopped onion	125 mL	1/2 cup
Garlic clove, minced	1	1
Ginger marmalade	50 mL	3 tbsp.
Tomato paste	30 mL	2 tbsp.
Chilli paste (sambal oelek)	4 mL	3/4 tsp.
Ground cinnamon	1 mL	1/4 tsp.
Ground cumin	1 mL	1/4 tsp.
Garlic bulbs, roasted (see How To, below)	2	2
Long baguette bread slices, toasted	8	8
Cambozola cheese (or mild blue cheese)	113 g	4 oz.

Heat olive oil in a frying pan on medium. Add onion and garlic and cook for about 5 minutes until onion is softened.

Add next 5 ingredients and stir until heated through. Transfer to a serving bowl.

Arrange remaining 3 ingredients on a serving platter with jam. Serves 4.

1 serving: 1221 Kilojoules (292 Calories); 16.0 g Total Fat (2.7 g Mono, 0.5 g Poly, 7.6 g Sat); 30 mg Cholesterol; 30 g Carbohydrate; 2 g Fibre; 7 g Protein; 318 mg Sodium

ABOUT CAMBOZOLA
Cambozola is a blue cheese that was developed in Germany in the 1970s. A cross between Camembert and Gorgonzola, Cambozola is a soft cheese with a notably smooth, creamy texture and light blue veins. It has a mild flavour, unlike the strong pungent sharpness of Stilton or Gorgonzola.

HOW TO ROAST GARLIC
To roast garlic, trim 6 mm (1/4 inch) from each bulb to expose tops of cloves, leaving bulbs intact. Wrap bulbs individually in greased foil and bake in 190°C (375°F) for about 45 minutes until tender. Let stand until cool enough to handle.

What makes this dish so **conversational** is the **interesting** use of tortilla shells to create toasty little cups. Be as **inventive** as you like and **create** your own fillings.

Potato Crostini
with Caramelised Bacon

Baby potatoes, ends trimmed and cut in half crosswise	8	8
Olive oil	15 mL	1 tbsp.
Salt	1 mL	1/4 tsp.
Brown sugar	125 mL	1/2 cup
Dried crushed chillies	5 mL	1 tsp.
Bacon slices	10	10
Sour cream	60 mL	1/4 cup
Cream cheese, softened	30 mL	2 tbsp.
Dijon mustard	2 mL	1/2 tsp.
Dried crushed chillies	1 mL	1/4 tsp.

Toss first 3 ingredients together in a bowl, then spread evenly on a baking tray. Bake in a 205°C (400°F) oven for about 25 minutes until potatoes are tender. Arrange potatoes, trimmed-side down, on a serving plate. Reduce oven temperature to 175°C (350°F).

Combine brown sugar and first amount of chillies. Coat bacon slices with the brown sugar mixture. Arrange on a wire rack set in a foil-lined baking tray. Bake for about 25 minutes until browned and glazed. Let stand for 10 minutes before finely chopping bacon.

Combine remaining 4 ingredients and bacon. Spoon onto potatoes. Makes 16 potato crostini.

1 potato crostini: 565 Kilojoules (135 Calories); 3.9 g Total Fat (1.7 g Mono, 0.4 g Poly, 1.5 g Sat); 8 mg Cholesterol; 22 g Carbohydrate; 2 g Fibre; 4 g Protein; 145 mg Sodium

---

GARNISH
Sprigs of parsley

Roasted baby potatoes make for an **interesting twist** on traditional bread crostini. **Caramelising** the bacon adds sweetness to the **smokiness**. Try using a combination of red and white potatoes for an appealing **colour** contrast.

Five-spiced Crepes
with Coconut Scallops

Large egg	1	1
Milk	125 mL	1/2 cup
Plain flour	100 mL	6 tbsp.
Butter, melted	25 mL	1 1/2 tbsp.
Granulated sugar	2 mL	1/2 tsp.
Chinese five-spice powder	1 mL	1/4 tsp.
Cooking oil	7 mL	1 1/2 tsp.
Sesame oil	10 mL	2 tsp.
Coarsely chopped scallops	250 mL	1 cup
Chopped spring onion	30 mL	2 tbsp.
Seasoned salt	2 mL	1/2 tsp.
Coconut milk	125 mL	1/2 cup
Cornflour	5 mL	1 tsp.

Using a blender or food processor, process first 6 ingredients until smooth. Let stand for 30 minutes.

Heat 1 mL (1/4 tsp.) cooking oil in a small frying pan on medium. Pour about 30 mL (2 tbsp.) batter into pan. Immediately tilt and swirl pan to ensure bottom is covered. Cook for about 1 minute until brown spots appear. Transfer to a plate. Repeat with remaining batter, heating cooking oil between batches to prevent sticking. Fold crepes into quarters and arrange on a serving plate.

Heat sesame oil in the same frying pan on medium. Add next 3 ingredients and cook for 1 minute. Combine coconut milk and cornflour and add to the pan. Heat and stir for about 1 minute until scallops are opaque and sauce is bubbling. Spoon over crepes. Serves 6.

1 serving: 716 Kilojoules (171 Calories); 11.1 g Total Fat (2.6 g Mono, 1.3 g Poly, 6.3 g Sat); 52 mg Cholesterol; 9 g Carbohydrate; trace Fibre; 9 g Protein; 222 mg Sodium

---

GARNISH
Toasted sesame seeds
Spring onion

ABOUT CHINESE FIVE-SPICE POWDER
This popular spice blend is used extensively in Chinese cooking. A pungent mixture of five different spices, usually cinnamon, cloves, fennel seed, star anise and Szechuan peppercorns, its flavour is quite distinct. You should easily find five-spice powder in your grocery store or specialty market.

An **exotic** and **intriguing** flavour experience. The scent of **aromatic spices** will give your guests just a **hint** of what they are about to **enjoy**.

Pear Puff Tart

Packet of puff pastry (397 g, 14 oz.), thawed according to packet directions	1/2	1/2
Granulated sugar	15 mL	1 tbsp.
Crumbled Stilton cheese	125 mL	1/2 cup
Medium fresh unpeeled pear, thinly sliced	1	1
Butter, melted	5 mL	1 tsp.
Coarsely ground pepper, sprinkle		

Roll out pastry to a 18 x 28 cm (7 x 11 inch) rectangle and transfer to a baking tray. Sprinkle with sugar.

Sprinkle with cheese, leaving a 12 mm (1/2 inch) border. Arrange pear slices over cheese. Brush with butter and sprinkle with pepper. Bake in a 205°C (400°F) oven for 20 to 25 minutes until golden. Cut into 8 pieces.

1 piece: 770 Kilojoules (184 Calories); 12.1 g Total Fat (5.5 g Mono, 1.2 g Poly, 3.9 g Sat); 8 mg Cholesterol; 16 g Carbohydrate; 1 g Fibre; 3 g Protein; 160 mg Sodium

ABOUT STILTON
Stilton is one of Britain's most well-known cheeses. Made from whole cow's milk, its sharp, nutty flavour strengthens during the four to six months it ages before being sold. Stilton is creamy and crumbly with a pale yellow interior, blue-green veins and a crusty brownish rind. White Stilton is also available. It is not aged as long, so no veins develop.

A perfect **combination** of sweet and savoury **flavours** on a bed of golden, buttery **pastry**. For a different **presentation**, serve the tart whole and allow your guests to cut their own **portions**.

Seafood
with Horseradish Beetroot Coulis

Uncooked extra-large prawns (shrimp; peeled and deveined)	12	12
Steak spice	5 mL	1 tsp.
Olive oil	10 mL	2 tsp.
Can of whole baby beetroots, puréed with 3 tbsp. (50 mL) juice	398 mL	14 oz.
Butter, melted	30 mL	2 tbsp.
Prepared horseradish	15 mL	1 tbsp.
Chopped fresh dill	10 mL	2 tsp.
Rocket, lightly packed	60 mL	1/4 cup

Combine prawns and steak spice. Let stand for 15 minutes. Heat olive oil in a frying pan on medium. Add prawns and cook until pink.

Combine next 4 ingredients and pour onto a serving plate.

Arrange rocket and prawns over top. Serves 4.

1 serving: 510 Kilojoules (122 Calories); 8.4 g Total Fat (3.2 g Mono, 0.6 g Poly, 4.0 g Sat); 47 mg Cholesterol; 7 g Carbohydrate; 1 g Fibre; 5 g Protein; 484 mg Sodium

---

> **HOW TO DEVEIN PRAWNS (SHRIMP)**
> To devein prawns, strip off the legs and peel away the shell. Using a small, sharp knife, make a shallow cut along the centre of the back. Rinse under cold water to wash out the dark vein.

A feast for the eyes and the palate with strong, bold flavours and vibrant colours – perfect for a sophisticated get-together.

Grecian Beef Pastries

Olive oil	5 mL	1 tsp.
Lean beef mince	225 g	1/2 lb.
Chopped red onion	125 mL	1/2 cup
Chopped red capsicum (bell pepper)	125 mL	1/2 cup
Sun-dried tomato pesto	30 mL	2 tbsp.
Lemon juice	10 mL	2 tsp.
Garlic clove, minced	1	1
Salt	1 mL	1/4 tsp.
Pepper	2 mL	1/2 tsp.
Grated lemon zest	5 mL	1 tsp.
Packet of puff pastry (397 g, 14 oz.), thawed according to packet directions	1/2	1/2
Chopped pitted kalamata olives	60 mL	1/4 cup
Crumbled feta cheese	125 mL	1/2 cup
Chopped fresh oregano	15 mL	1 tbsp.

Heat olive oil in a frying pan on medium. Add next 8 ingredients and scramble-fry until beef is no longer pink. Remove from heat.

Stir in lemon zest and let stand until cool.

Roll out pastry to a 30 x 30 cm (12 x 12 inch) square. Cut into 12 rectangles and transfer to a greased baking tray. Sprinkle with beef mixture, leaving a 6 mm (1/4 inch) border. Press down gently.

Sprinkle with olives and cheese. Bake in a 205°C (400°F) oven for about 20 minutes until pastry and cheese are golden.

Sprinkle with oregano. Makes 12 pastries.

1 pastry: 690 Kilojoules (165 Calories); 11.0 g Total Fat (5.6 g Mono, 1.0 g Poly, 3.7 g Sat); 17 mg Cholesterol; 10 g Carbohydrate; 1 g Fibre; 6 g Protein; 304 mg Sodium

---

GARNISH
Lemon wedges

TIP
Be sure to add fresh herbs at the end of cooking or as a garnish for maximum flavour impact.

EXPERIMENT!
Vary the flavour and make it with lamb instead of beef. You could also try seasoned or marinated feta instead of plain.

Opa! Make it a completely Greek experience by serving a rich red wine or a shot of ouzo with these sensational little pastries.

Complex. There is much ado about small plates, but not all scrumptious fare sits on the surface. Rich treasures lie in bowls and are worth digging for. Pick up a fork or spoon and see what you can unearth. Delicious plunder is ready to be discovered in these pots of gourmet gold. Dishes with such depth truly need to be explored and experienced.

Little Bowls

Heady dips, hot and cold soups, rich risottos and succulent mélanges

Panini Sticks
with Dipping Trio

Ingredient	Metric	Imperial
Extra virgin olive oil	15 mL	1 tbsp.
Finely chopped fresh rosemary	5 mL	1 tsp.
Dried marjoram, crushed	5 mL	1 tsp.
Square panini breads (20 x 20 cm, 8 x 8 inches, each)	2	2
Coarse salt, sprinkle		
SUN-DRIED TOMATO DIP		
Tzatziki sauce	75 mL	1/3 cup
Sun-dried tomato pesto	10 mL	2 tsp.
Chilli paste (sambal oelek)	1 mL	1/4 tsp.
LEMON AIOLI DIP		
Roasted garlic mayonnaise	75 mL	1/3 cup
Lemon juice	10 mL	2 tsp.
Grated lemon zest	5 mL	1 tsp.
TZATZIKI HERB DIP		
Tzatziki sauce	75 mL	1/3 cup
Chopped fresh dill	7 mL	1 1/2 tsp.
Chopped fresh mint	7 mL	1 1/2 tsp.
Lemon pepper	2 mL	1/2 tsp.

Combine first 3 ingredients and brush on panini breads. Cut into 2.5 cm (1 inch) wide strips and arrange, close together, on a baking tray. Sprinkle with salt. Bake in a 205°C (400°F) oven for about 8 minutes until edges are crisp.

Sun-dried Tomato Dip: Combine all 3 ingredients.

Lemon Aioli Dip: Combine all 3 ingredients.

Tzatziki Herb Dip: Combine all 4 ingredients.

Serve dips with panini sticks. Serves 8.

1 serving: 929 Kilojoules (222 Calories); 15.4 g Total Fat (3.2 g Mono, 4.1 g Poly, 1.8 g Sat); 13 mg Cholesterol; 31 g Carbohydrate; 1 g Fibre; 3 g Protein; 366 mg Sodium

---

GARNISH
Sprig of basil
Lemon peel
Sprig of mint

PRESENTATION INSPIRATION
Provide individual plates so guests can serve themselves a spoonful of each dip. This way guests can sample all three – and it will help to avoid the temptation to double-dip!

Sometimes picking up a **convenience** product and adding a few simple **embellishments** is all it takes to truly make it your own. This very shareable **treat** is just as easy to make as it is to **enjoy**.

Seafood Bisque

Butter	15 mL	1 tbsp.
Uncooked medium prawns (shrimp; peeled and deveined), tails intact	6	6
Finely chopped celery	60 mL	1/4 cup
Finely chopped shallots	60 mL	1/4 cup
Uncooked prawns (shrimp; peeled and deveined), chopped	85 g	3 oz.
Can of tomato purée (tomato paste)	213 mL	7 1/2 oz.
Pouring cream	75 mL	1/3 cup
Dry white wine	60 mL	1/4 cup
Chopped fresh tarragon	2 mL	1/2 tsp.
Fresh tarragon leaves	6	6

Melt butter in a saucepan on medium. Add first amount of prawns and cook until pink. Transfer to a plate and set aside.

Add celery and shallots to the same saucepan and cook for about 5 minutes until softened.

Stir in next 5 ingredients. Simmer, covered, on medium-low for 5 minutes. Using a hand blender, process until smooth (see Safety Tip, below). Pour into 6 small serving cups.

Place 1 prawn and 1 tarragon leaf over each cup of soup. Serves 6.

1 serving: 435 Kilojoules (104 Calories); 6.9 g Total Fat (1.9 g Mono, 0.4 g Poly, 4.2 g Sat); 53 mg Cholesterol; 4 g Carbohydrate; 1 g Fibre; 5 g Protein; 268 mg Sodium

---

SAFETY TIP
We recommend that you not use a countertop blender to process hot liquids.

ABOUT PRAWNS (SHRIMP)
Prawns are sold according to size, but keep in mind that the perception of size varies from region to region, as well as between fish markets. As a general guideline, these are the number of prawns you can expect to get from a 454 g (1 lb.) measure:

- Jumbo   11–15
- Extra-large   16–20
- Large   21–30
- Medium   31–35
- Small   36–45
- Baby (or shrimps) about 100

Elegant and rich-tasting bisque is most satisfying when sampled in small portions. These little bowls truly taste like traditional bisque, but take much less time to prepare.

Sun-dried Tomato and Leek Mussels

Mussels	454 g	1 lb.
Olive oil	7 mL	1 1/2 tsp.
Finely chopped leek (white part only)	125 mL	1/2 cup
Garlic clove, minced	1	1
Dried crushed chillies	0.5 mL	1/8 tsp.
Dry white wine	175 mL	3/4 cup
Sun-dried tomato pesto	30 mL	2 tbsp.

Lightly tap to close any mussels that are opened 6 mm (1/4 inch) or more. Discard any that do not close.

Heat olive oil in a saucepan on medium. Add next 3 ingredients and cook for about 5 minutes until leek is softened.

Stir in wine and pesto. Bring to the boil and add mussels. Cook, covered, for about 5 minutes until mussels are opened. Discard any unopened mussels. Serves 4.

NOTE: For safety reasons, it is important to discard any mussels that do not close before cooking, as well as any that have not opened during cooking.

1 serving: 410 Kilojoules (98 Calories); 2.4 g Total Fat (1.4 g Mono, 0.4 g Poly, 0.4 g Sat); 8 mg Cholesterol; 7 g Carbohydrate; 1 g Fibre; 4 g Protein; 406 mg Sodium

---

GARNISH
Chopped fresh chives

ABOUT MUSSELS
When cooking with mussels, there are a few points to keep in mind:

- Use only mussels with tightly closed shells. If the shells are slightly open, tap them lightly. If they don't close, don't cook them.
- Discard any mussels with broken shells.
- Avoid mussels that feel heavy, as they are often filled with sand.
- Don't use mussels that feel too light or loose when shaken.
- Shucked mussels should be plump, with clear liquid.
- Smaller mussels tend to be more tender than larger ones.
- Discard any mussels that do not open during cooking.

Plump, juicy **mussels** bathe in a pesto, wine and leek **sauce**. Serve with **crusty** French bread for **dipping**.

Smoked Salmon Blintz Cups

Ricotta cheese	125 mL	1/2 cup
Chopped smoked salmon	60 mL	1/4 cup
Cream cheese, softened	60 mL	1/4 cup
Chopped fresh dill	15 mL	1 tbsp.
Pepper	1 mL	1/4 tsp.
Plain flour	250 mL	1 cup
Baking powder	5 mL	1 tsp.
Salt	1 mL	1/4 tsp
Large eggs	3	3
Milk	75 mL	1/3 cup
Butter, melted	30 mL	2 tbsp.
Granulated sugar	30 mL	2 tbsp.

Combine first 5 ingredients. Set aside.

Combine next 3 ingredients in a small bowl. Make a well in the centre.

Whisk next 4 ingredients in a separate bowl and add to the well. Whisk until smooth. Pour about 60 mL (1/4 cup) batter into each of 6 greased 170 mL (6 oz.) ramekins. Carefully spoon salmon mixture over batter. Pour remaining batter over top. Bake in a 175°C (350°F) oven for 15 to 18 minutes until slightly puffed but firm to the touch. Let stand for 5 minutes before removing blintz cups from ramekins to a serving plate. Makes 6 blintz cups.

1 blintz cup: 950 Kilojoules (227 Calories); 11.6 g Total Fat (3.6 g Mono, 0.7 g Poly, 6.4 g Sat); 122 mg Cholesterol; 21 g Carbohydrate; trace Fibre; 10 g Protein; 299 mg Sodium

---

GARNISH
Sprigs of fresh dill
Red capsicum (bell pepper) slivers

ABOUT GARNISHING
Why garnish? It's sad to say, but not all food looks as good as it tastes. Garnishing helps to add a little bit of extra colour or artistic flair to your food. Garnishes don't always have to be placed directly on your food either. Sometimes they can be placed underneath or around the food, decorating the plate itself. Keep in mind that a garnish should not only be attractive, it should also reflect the flavours of the dish you're serving it with. That way, your guests get a hint about what flavours to expect.

Blintzes are known for being labour-intensive, but we've found a great way to make them without all the fuss. Creamy smoked salmon filling hides inside a rich, golden batter for an unforgettable flavour.

Mango Gazpacho

Chopped mango (see Tip, below)	250 mL	1 cup
Orange juice	75 mL	1/3 cup
Chopped fresh coriander	15 mL	1 tbsp.
Lime juice	15 mL	1 tbsp.
Brown sugar	2 mL	1/2 tsp.
Finely grated fresh ginger	2 mL	1/2 tsp.
Ground cumin	2 mL	1/2 tsp.
Salt	2 mL	1/2 tsp.
Pepper	0.5 mL	1/8 tsp.
Diced English cucumber (with peel)	60 mL	1/4 cup
Diced mango	60 mL	1/4 cup
Diced red capsicum (bell pepper)	60 mL	1/4 cup

In a blender or food processor, process first 9 ingredients until smooth.

Stir in remaining 3 ingredients. Chill, covered, for about 1 hour until cold. Pour into 4 small serving cups. Serves 4.

1 serving: 213 Kilojoules (51 Calories); 0.3 g Total Fat (0.1 g Mono, 0.1 g Poly, 0.1 g Sat); 0 mg Cholesterol; 13 g Carbohydrate; 1 g Fibre; 1 g Protein; 295 mg Sodium

TIP
For faster prep, use frozen mango. Chop it up while it's still icy and you'll save time on the chill factor.

ABOUT GAZPACHO
Originating from southern Spain, gazpacho's conventional form usually contains tomatoes. Served cold, this refreshing puréed soup can be either smooth or chunky. Today, there are many versions of this elegant dish – including sweeter ones.

A cool, upbeat take on gazpacho. Mango is the hero in this chilled soup with coriander as the sidekick. There's something distinctively modern about the pairing of these two flavours.

Coconut Chilli Soup

Sesame oil	10 mL	2 tsp.
Finely chopped onion	125 mL	1/2 cup
Garlic clove, minced	1	1
Thai red curry paste	2 mL	1/2 tsp.
Coconut milk	250 mL	1 cup
Prepared vegetable stock (broth)	125 mL	1/2 cup
Brown sugar	5 mL	1 tsp.
Soy sauce	5 mL	1 tsp.
Lime juice	4 mL	3/4 tsp.

Heat sesame oil in a saucepan on medium. Add next 3 ingredients and cook for about 5 minutes until onion is softened.

Stir in next 4 ingredients. Simmer, covered, for 10 minutes to blend flavours. Remove from heat.

Stir in lime juice. Using a hand blender, process until smooth (see Safety Tip, page 34). Strain into 4 small serving bowls and discard solids. Serves 4.

1 serving: 661 Kilojoules (158 Calories); 15.2 g Total Fat (1.4 g Mono, 1.1 g Poly, 11.7 g Sat); 0 mg Cholesterol; 6 g Carbohydrate; trace Fibre; 1.7 g Protein; 155 mg Sodium

---

GARNISH
Thai hot chillies
Hot chilli oil

Transport yourself to the **tropics** with this smooth, **velvety** soup. The intensity comes from Thai red **curry** paste – just enough to really **heat** things up.

Butter Chicken
with Spinach and Pappadums

Tandoori curry paste	50 mL	3 tbsp.
Boneless, skinless chicken thighs, chopped	225 g	1/2 lb.
Butter	15 mL	1 tbsp.
Chopped onion	250 mL	1 cup
Diced Roma (plum) tomato	175 mL	3/4 cup
Butter	15 mL	1 tbsp.
Pouring cream	125 mL	1/2 cup
Chopped fresh spinach leaves, lightly packed	250 mL	1 cup
Chopped fresh coriander	15 mL	1 tbsp.
Sliced almonds, toasted (see How To, page 178)	15 mL	1 tbsp.
Black peppercorn or plain pappadums	8	8
Cooking spray		

Combine curry paste and chicken. Melt butter in a frying pan on medium. Add onion and chicken mixture and cook for about 10 minutes until onion is soft.

Add tomato and second amount of butter and cook until tomato is soft. Stir in cream. Simmer for about 10 minutes until thickened and reduced by half.

Stir in spinach and cook until wilted. Transfer to a serving bowl and sprinkle with coriander and almonds.

Spray both sides of pappadums with cooking spray. Grill, 2 at a time, for about 30 seconds until puffed. Turn pappadums. Grill for about 10 seconds until golden. Serve with chicken. Serves 4.

1 serving: 1348 Kilojoules (322 Calories); 26.9 g Total Fat (6.9 g Mono, 1.9 g Poly, 12.2 g Sat); 90 mg Cholesterol; 14 g Carbohydrate; 2 g Fibre; 13 g Protein; 493 mg Sodium

---

EXPERIMENT!
Pappadums come in a variety of flavours. Try experimenting with different types for this recipe. Some flavours you might find in your grocery store or specialty food store include:

- Plain
- Garlic
- Cumin
- Sesame
- Coriander
- Green chilli
- Corn
- Red chilli

Transport yourself to the **tropics** with this smooth, **velvety** soup. The intensity comes from Thai red **curry** paste – just enough to really **heat** things up.

Miso Mushroom Risotto
with Scallops

Sesame oil	10 mL	2 tsp.
Chopped fresh shiitake mushrooms	500 mL	2 cups
Chopped spring onion	60 mL	1/4 cup
Dry white wine	75 mL	1/3 cup
White miso	15 mL	1 tbsp.
Arborio rice	125 mL	1/2 cup
Water	325 mL	1 1/3 cups
Salt	2 mL	1/2 tsp.
Sesame oil	10 mL	2 tsp.
Large sea scallops	4	4
Sea salt	2 mL	1/2 tsp.

Heat first amount of sesame oil in a saucepan on medium. Add mushrooms and spring onion and cook for about 8 minutes until mushrooms are browned.

Stir in wine and miso and cook until wine is almost all evaporated. Add rice and stir for 30 seconds.

Stir in water and salt. Bring to the boil. Simmer, covered, on medium-low for about 20 minutes, without stirring, until rice is tender. Let stand, covered, for 5 minutes.

Heat second amount of sesame oil in a frying pan on medium. Add scallops, sprinkle with sea salt and cook for about 3 minutes until scallops are opaque and browned. Stir risotto and divide into 4 small bowls, placing 1 scallop over top. Serves 4.

1 serving: 791 Kilojoules (189 Calories); 5.4 g Total Fat (1.9 g Mono, 2.2 g Poly, 0.9 g Sat); 5 mg Cholesterol; 26 g Carbohydrate; 1 g Fibre; 7 g Protein; 738 mg Sodium

---

GARNISH
Fresh chives

MAKE AHEAD
The risotto reheats well in the microwave, so it can be made in advance.

PRESENTATION INSPIRATION
Try serving the risotto in Asian-themed or small, square bowls. Have chopsticks available for your guests, but provide forks as well for any guests who lack confidence in their chopstick skills.

Get the conversation started with this **fascinating** sampling of **fusion cuisine**. Asian flavours of sesame and miso meet Italian risotto for an **intriguing union** of cultural cookery.

Butter Chicken
with Spinach and Pappadums

Tandoori curry paste	50 mL	3 tbsp.
Boneless, skinless chicken thighs, chopped	225 g	1/2 lb.
Butter	15 mL	1 tbsp.
Chopped onion	250 mL	1 cup
Diced Roma (plum) tomato	175 mL	3/4 cup
Butter	15 mL	1 tbsp.
Pouring cream	125 mL	1/2 cup
Chopped fresh spinach leaves, lightly packed	250 mL	1 cup
Chopped fresh coriander	15 mL	1 tbsp.
Sliced almonds, toasted (see How To, page 178)	15 mL	1 tbsp.
Black peppercorn or plain pappadums	8	8
Cooking spray		

Combine curry paste and chicken. Melt butter in a frying pan on medium. Add onion and chicken mixture and cook for about 10 minutes until onion is soft.

Add tomato and second amount of butter and cook until tomato is soft. Stir in cream. Simmer for about 10 minutes until thickened and reduced by half.

Stir in spinach and cook until wilted. Transfer to a serving bowl and sprinkle with coriander and almonds.

Spray both sides of pappadums with cooking spray. Grill, 2 at a time, for about 30 seconds until puffed. Turn pappadums. Grill for about 10 seconds until golden. Serve with chicken. Serves 4.

1 serving: 1348 Kilojoules (322 Calories); 26.9 g Total Fat (6.9 g Mono, 1.9 g Poly, 12.2 g Sat); 90 mg Cholesterol; 14 g Carbohydrate; 2 g Fibre; 13 g Protein; 493 mg Sodium

---

EXPERIMENT!
Pappadums come in a variety of flavours. Try experimenting with different types for this recipe. Some flavours you might find in your grocery store or specialty food store include:

- Plain
- Garlic
- Cumin
- Sesame
- Coriander
- Green chilli
- Corn
- Red chilli

Crisp pappacums make the perfect base for serving miniature portions of this popular Indian entrée. Consider serving this dish with samosas or Curried Cheese and Fruit Wheel (page 194) and Walnut Ginger Crisps (page 68).

Rebellious. Some things are just too original to be classified. These small plates defy tidy categories – and that puts them in a class of their own. Familiar dishes done new ways – like 'Uptown' Goat Cheese Potato Skins or Crab Sushi Squares – are beguiling. Vibrant, daring, unique and sometimes entirely unexpected, these wickedly delicious bites are bound to thrill. You can't help it; the attraction is undeniable. Everyone secretly roots for the rebel.

Maverick Morsels

Inspired twists on favourite flavours

Seared Beef Carpaccio
with Peppercorn Mushrooms

Steak spice	15 mL	1 tbsp.
Chopped fresh thyme	15 mL	1 tbsp.
Beef strip or top loin steak	454 g	1 lb.
Cooking oil	15 mL	1 tbsp.
Sliced brown mushrooms	1.25 L	5 cups
Brandy	75 mL	1/3 cup
Canned green peppercorns	15 mL	1 tbsp.
Butter	15 ml	1 tbsp.
Rocket, lightly packed	125 mL	1/2 cup

Combine steak spice and thyme. Press steak into spice mixture until coated. Cook on a greased grill pan on high for about 2 minutes per side until browned and slightly crisp. Transfer to cutting board. Cover with foil and let stand for 10 minutes.

Heat cooking oil in a frying pan on medium-high. Add mushrooms and cook until browned and liquid is evaporated.

Stir in brandy and peppercorns. Add butter and stir until melted.

Cut steak across the grain into very thin slices. Arrange with rocket and mushrooms on a serving plate. Serves 6.

1 serving: 1046 Kilojoules (250 Calories); 15.7 g Total Fat (6.7 g Mono, 1.2 g Poly, 6.0 g Sat); 47 mg Cholesterol; 3 g Carbohydrate; 1 g Fibre; 17 g Protein; 391 mg Sodium

ALTERNATIVE METHOD
Instead of grilling the steak, you can sear it, using olive oil, in a very hot stainless steel or cast iron frying pan. Sear each side for only one minute. The result will be a very thin, dark crust that is quite appealing. However, it is not recommended that you use this method with a non-stick pan, as the high heat may ruin the non-stick coating.

Satiate your senses. Peppery, thinly sliced beef and mushrooms sautéed in **brandy** and **green peppercorns** unite with the natural zing of rocket.

Peanut Noodle Cakes
with Sweet Chilli Seafood

Ingredient	Metric	Imperial
Uncooked large prawns (shrimp; peeled and deveined), butterflied (see How To, below), tails intact	12	12
Sweet chilli sauce	75 mL	1/3 cup
Water	50 mL	3 tbsp.
Soy sauce	15 mL	1 tbsp.
Large egg	1	1
Chunky peanut butter	15 mL	1 tbsp.
Thai red curry paste	7 mL	1 1/2 tsp.
Cooked spaghettini	500 mL	2 cups
Chopped fresh coriander	30 mL	2 tbsp.
Chopped spring onion	30 mL	2 tbsp.
Cooking oil	50 mL	3 tbsp.

Toss first 4 ingredients together in a bowl. Let stand for 10 minutes.

Whisk next 3 ingredients together in a medium bowl. Add next 3 ingredients. Toss together until well coated.

Heat cooking oil in a large frying pan on medium. Make 6 rounds of noodle mixture in the pan. Cook for about 5 minutes per side, pressing lightly to flatten, until crispy and golden. Transfer to a plate. Add prawn mixture to the same frying pan and cook on medium-high for about 2 minutes until prawns turn pink. Place 2 prawns over each noodle cake and drizzle with pan juices. Serves 6.

1 serving: 837 Kilojoules (200 Calories); 9.9 g Total Fat (5.1 g Mono, 2.8 g Poly, 1.2 g Sat); 52 mg Cholesterol; 20 g Carbohydrate; 1 g Fibre; 7 g Protein; 646 mg Sodium

HOW TO BUTTERFLY PRAWNS (SHRIMP)

GARNISH
Chopped fresh coriander
Salted peanuts
Lime wedges

Sure to spark applause and lively conversation, these curiosity-piquing noodle cakes will delight the cook as much in cooking as they delight the guests in indulging.

'Uptown' Goat Cheese Potato Skins

Medium unpeeled baking potatoes, baked and cooled	3	3
Olive oil	30 mL	2 tbsp.
Lemon pepper	2 mL	1/2 tsp.
Crumbled goat (chèvre) cheese	175 mL	3/4 cup
Grated havarti cheese	125 mL	1/2 cup
Butter	15 mL	1 tbsp.
Coarsely chopped capers	50 mL	3 tbsp.
Garlic cloves, thinly sliced	2	2
Sun-dried tomatoes in oil, blotted dry and finely chopped	75 mL	1/3 cup
Chopped fresh chives	30 mL	2 tbsp.
Chopped fresh oregano	15 mL	1 tbsp.

Cut potatoes into quarters lengthwise. Scoop away pulp, leaving a thin layer on each skin. Brush both sides of skins with olive oil and sprinkle with lemon pepper. Place, skin-side up, on a baking tray. Bake in a 220°C (425°F) oven for about 7 minutes until starting to crisp. Turn over.

Sprinkle goat and havarti cheese over top. Bake for about 7 minutes until cheese is melted and golden. Arrange on a serving platter.

Melt butter in a frying pan on medium. Add capers and garlic and cook for about 5 minutes until garlic is golden. Spoon over potatoes.

Sprinkle with remaining 3 ingredients. Makes 12 potato skins.

1 potato skin: 531 Kilojoules (127 Calories); 8.7 g Total Fat (2.4 g Mono, 0.3 g Poly, 4.7 g Sat); 15 mg Cholesterol; 7 g Carbohydrate; 1 g Fibre; 5 g Protein; 219 mg Sodium

---

TIME SAVER
Feel free to bake the potatoes a day in advance. Cooking the potatoes in the microwave is another option for added convenience. Just prick the potatoes in several places with a fork and wrap individually with paper towel. Microwave on high (100%) for 8 to 10 minutes until tender, turning the potatoes halfway through cooking.

Potato skins, not often invited to the better parties, become *de rigueur* as showier fare when melded with the rich and complementary flavours of lemon, capers and chèvre.

Sweet Polenta Fries
with Jalapeño Lime Dip

Sour cream	60 mL	1/4 cup
Mayonnaise	60 mL	1/4 cup
Lime juice	30 mL	2 tbsp.
Chopped fresh coriander	30 mL	2 tbsp.
Finely chopped jalapeño chillies and smoky barbecue sauce (see Tip, page 172)	7 mL	1 1/2 tsp.
Grated lime zest	2 mL	1/2 tsp.
Coarse (sanding) sugar	60 mL	1/4 cup
Coarse sea salt	30 mL	2 tbsp.
Ground cumin	15 mL	1 tbsp.
Ground coriander	7 mL	1 1/2 tsp.
Cayenne pepper	2 mL	1/2 tsp.
Polenta roll (or cooked polenta shaped into a roll)	500 g	1.1 lb.
Plain flour	60 mL	1/4 cup
Cooking oil	750 mL	3 cups

Combine first 6 ingredients. Set aside.

Combine next 5 ingredients. Set aside.

Cut polenta roll into fries, about 12 mm (1/2 inch) thick. Gently toss in flour until coated.

Heat cooking oil in a large frying pan on medium-high (see How To, page 106). Shallow-fry polenta in batches, for about 5 minutes per batch, until golden. Transfer with a slotted spoon to paper towels to drain. While fries are still hot, toss with 15 mL (1 tbsp.) sugar mixture until coated. Serve with dip and remaining sugar mixture. Serves 6.

1 serving: 1088 Kilojoules (260 Calories); 15.9 g Total Fat (8.5 g Mono, 4.4 g Poly, 2.1 g Sat); 7 mg Cholesterol; 27 g Carbohydrate; 1 g Fibre; 3 g Protein; 2691 mg Sodium

TIP
Tossing items in flour before frying helps prevent them from sticking to each other.

ABOUT SANDING SUGAR
Sanding, or coarse, sugar tastes the same as granulated sugar – its difference lies purely in aesthetics. Because the sugar grain is larger, it sparkles or glints, giving an eye-catching appearance to whatever it's used on. It comes in a variety of colours – although the bright hues are more suited to desserts or confections.

Let your guests enjoy the interactive experience of dredging these unique polenta fries in a sweet and spicy seasoning before taking them for a dunk in the perfectly complementary dip.

Walnut Pesto-crusted Lamb
with Cranberry Port Jus

Ingredient	Metric	Imperial
Rack of lamb (8 ribs), bones Frenched (see Tip, below)	1	1
Salt, sprinkle		
Pepper, sprinkle		
Cooking oil	5 mL	1 tsp.
Ruby port	250 mL	1 cup
Cranberries	125 mL	1/2 cup
Balsamic vinegar	10 mL	2 tsp.
Wholemeal bread slice	1	1
Chopped walnuts, toasted (see How To, page 178)	30 mL	2 tbsp.
Basil pesto	5 mL	1 tsp.
Butter, melted	15 mL	1 tbsp.
Dijon mustard	15 mL	1 tbsp.

Cover bones of lamb rack with foil (see Tip, below). Sprinkle with salt and pepper. Heat cooking oil in a frying pan on medium-high. Sear lamb until browned. Transfer to a plate.

Add port and cranberries to the same frying pan. Boil gently until reduced by half. Stir in vinegar. Transfer to a blender or food processor and process until smooth.

In a clean blender or food processor, process bread into coarse crumbs. Add walnuts and pesto and process until just combined. Transfer to a bowl. Drizzle with butter and toss until combined.

Brush meaty side of lamb with mustard. Press crumb mixture over the mustard. Bake, uncovered, in a 190°C (375°F) oven for 20 to 25 minutes until internal temperature reaches 57°C (135°F) or until meat reaches desired doneness. Cover with foil and let stand for 10 minutes. Cut lamb rack into 1-bone portions and serve with cranberry mixture. Serves 8.

1 serving: 628 Kilojoules (150 Calories); 6.1 g Total Fat (2.0 g Mono, 1.4 g Poly, 2.2 g Sat); 30 mg Cholesterol; 7 g Carbohydrate; 1 g Fibre; 9 g Protein; 97 mg Sodium

---

TIP
When getting your lamb rack cut, ask the butcher to remove the chine bone (also known as the backbone). This will make the ribs much easier to slice and separate.

TIP
Cover any exposed bone with foil before roasting to help prevent darkening.

Delicate walnut-crusted chops in a fruity *jus* will tantalise and tease – just enough to caress the palate and still have it yearning for the next taste sensation.

Crab Sushi Squares

Japanese-style (sushi) rice	175 mL	3/4 cup
Water	250 mL	1 cup
Mirin	25 mL	1 1/2 tbsp.
Rice vinegar	25 mL	1 1/2 tbsp.
Granulated sugar	15 mL	1 tbsp.
Black sesame seeds (or toasted white sesame seeds)	2 mL	1/2 tsp.
Salt	2 mL	1/2 tsp.
Nori (roasted seaweed) sheet	1	1
Large ripe avocado, thinly sliced	1	1
Can of crabmeat squeezed dry, cartilage removed	320 g	11 oz.
Mayonnaise	50 mL	3 tbsp.
Chilli paste (sambal oelek)	5 mL	1 tsp.
Black sesame seeds, sprinkle		

Combine rice and water in a small saucepan. Bring to the boil. Simmer, covered, on medium-low for 20 minutes, without stirring. Remove from heat and let stand, covered, for 10 minutes. Transfer to a bowl.

Stir next 5 ingredients until sugar is dissolved. Add to rice and mix well. Line the bottom of an 20 x 20 cm (8 x 8 inch) baking dish with foil, allowing foil to overhang on opposite sides.

Place nori sheet in baking dish, cutting to fit if necessary. Firmly press rice mixture over nori.

Arrange avocado slices over top.

Combine next 3 ingredients and spread over avocado. Sprinkle with sesame seeds. Chill, covered, for 1 hour. Use overhanging foil to remove sushi from the baking dish (see How To, below) and cut into 16 squares.

1 square: 339 Kilojoules (81 Calories); 3.5 g Total Fat (2.0 g Mono, 0.7 g Poly, 0.4 g Sat); 1 mg Cholesterol; 9 g Carbohydrate; trace Fibre; 4 g Protein; 236 mg Sodium

HOW TO REMOVE SUSHI

GARNISH
Red capsicum (bell pepper) slivers Fresh coriander leaves

Crab Sushi Squares

Japanese-style (sushi) rice	175 mL	3/4 cup
Water	250 mL	1 cup
Mirin	25 mL	1 1/2 tbsp.
Rice vinegar	25 mL	1 1/2 tbsp.
Granulated sugar	15 mL	1 tbsp.
Black sesame seeds (or toasted white sesame seeds)	2 mL	1/2 tsp.
Salt	2 mL	1/2 tsp.
Nori (roasted seaweed) sheet	1	1
Large ripe avocado, thinly sliced	1	1
Can of crabmeat squeezed dry, cartilage removed	320 g	11 oz.
Mayonnaise	50 mL	3 tbsp.
Chilli paste (sambal oelek)	5 mL	1 tsp.
Black sesame seeds, sprinkle		

Combine rice and water in a small saucepan. Bring to the boil. Simmer, covered, on medium-low for 20 minutes, without stirring. Remove from heat and let stand, covered, for 10 minutes. Transfer to a bowl.

Stir next 5 ingredients until sugar is dissolved. Add to rice and mix well. Line the bottom of an 20 x 20 cm (8 x 8 inch) baking dish with foil, allowing foil to overhang on opposite sides.

Place nori sheet in baking dish, cutting to fit if necessary. Firmly press rice mixture over nori.

Arrange avocado slices over top.

Combine next 3 ingredients and spread over avocado. Sprinkle with sesame seeds. Chill, covered, for 1 hour. Use overhanging foil to remove sushi from the baking dish (see How To, below) and cut into 16 squares.

1 square: 339 Kilojoules (81 Calories); 3.5 g Total Fat (2.0 g Mono, 0.7 g Poly, 0.4 g Sat); 1 mg Cholesterol; 9 g Carbohydrate; trace Fibre; 4 g Protein; 236 mg Sodium

HOW TO REMOVE SUSHI

GARNISH
Red capsicum (bell pepper) slivers Fresh coriander leaves

You'll be **pleased** to bring these **drumettes** to your fiesta with their **exceptional** flavouring and **unique** presentation – your guests will be too **curious** to miss out.

Margarita Chicken Lollipops

Tequila	125 mL	1/2 cup
Lime juice	60 mL	1/4 cup
Dried crushed chillies	5 mL	1 tsp.
Ground cumin	5 mL	1 tsp.
Chilli powder	2 mL	1/2 tsp.
Garlic powder	2 mL	1/2 tsp.
Salt	2 mL	1/2 tsp.
Chicken drumettes, Frenched (optional), see How To, below	900 g	2 lb.
Cornflour	10 mL	2 tsp.
Tequila	30 mL	2 tbsp.
Orange juice	15 mL	1 tbsp.
Honey	15 mL	1 tbsp.
Grated lime zest	5 mL	1 tsp.

Combine first 7 ingredients in a large resealable freezer bag. Add drumettes and marinate for 4 hours. Drain marinade into a saucepan. Simmer on medium for 5 minutes.

Stir cornflour into tequila and orange juice. Add to simmering marinade mixture and stir until bubbling and thickened. Stir in honey and lime zest. Arrange drumettes on a foil-lined baking tray. Brush marinade mixture over drumettes. Bake in a 220°C (425°F) oven for about 20 minutes, brushing occasionally with marinade mixture, until no longer pink inside. Makes about 16 drumettes.

1 drumette: 678 Kilojoules (162 Calories); 9.1 g Total Fat (trace Mono, trace Poly, 2.4 Sat); 43 mg Cholesterol; 2 g Carbohydrate; trace Fibre; 10 g Protein; 117 mg Sodium

HOW TO FRENCH DRUMETTES
Use a sharp knife to loosen the meat and skin from the skinny end of the drumette. Gently push the skin and meat towards the fat end of the drumette, cleanly exposing the bone. Remove any bits of fat.

GARNISH
Lime wedges

Delicate walnut-crusted chops in a fruity *jus* will **tantalise** and **tease** – just enough to **caress** the palate and still have it **yearning** for the next taste **sensation**.

Experience sushi **layered** rather than rolled, for a familiar California roll flavour with a **unique** and **stylish** presentation. Accompany with **pickled ginger** or wasabi for the sushi enthusiasts in your crowd.

Savoury Shortbread Trio

Butter, room temperature	175 mL	3/4 cup
Icing (confectioner's) sugar	75 mL	1/3 cup
Plain flour	300 mL	1 1/4 cups
Salt	0.5 mL	1/8 tsp.
CHIVE, LEMON AND POPPY SEED SHORTBREAD		
Chopped fresh chives	30 mL	2 tbsp.
Grated lemon zest	5 mL	1 tsp.
Poppy seeds	5 mL	1 tsp.
PECAN, CURRY AND CORIANDER SHORTBREAD		
Chopped pecans, toasted (see How To, page 178)	15 mL	1 tbsp.
Finely chopped fresh coriander	5 mL	1 tsp.
Madras curry paste	5 mL	1 tsp.
PINE NUT, BASIL AND PEPPER SHORTBREAD		
Chopped pine nuts, toasted (see How To, page 178)	30 mL	2 tbsp.
Finely chopped fresh basil	15 mL	1 tbsp.
Coarsely ground pepper	1 mL	1/4 tsp.

Cream butter and sugar. Stir in flour and salt until no dry flour remains. Divide into 3 equal portions.

Chive, Lemon and Poppy Seed Shortbread: Stir all 3 ingredients into 1 portion of dough.

Pecan, Curry and Coriander Shortbread: Stir all 3 ingredients into 1 portion of dough.

Pine Nut, Basil and Pepper Shortbread: Stir all 3 ingredients into remaining portion of dough.

Roll each dough mixture into a 10 cm (4 inch) cylinder (see How To, below) and wrap individually with parchment paper. Chill for about 1 hour until firm. Cut into 6 mm (1/4 inch) thick slices and arrange on biscuit trays. Bake in a 150°C (300°F) oven for about 15 minutes until golden. Makes about 48 shortbread.

3 shortbread: 552 Kilojoules (132 Calories); 10.0 g Total Fat (2.8 g Mono, 0.8 g Poly, 5.6 g Sat); 23 mg Cholesterol; 10 g Carbohydrate; trace Fibre; 1 g Protein; 90 mg Sodium

HOW TO FORM PERFECT CYLINDERS
To create uniform cylinders, first shape the dough into a log with your hands. Place the dough on the centre of a sheet of parchment (or waxed) paper, about 20 cm (8 inches) long, and fold the top half of the plastic wrap and parchment paper over the dough. Holding the edge of the parchment paper, use a pastry scraper or ruler to push the paper crease under the roll. The dough will form a perfect cylinder for easy and uniform slicing.

Perfectly suited for an evening of wine-tasting, these three tempting variations of savoury shortbread will melt in your mouth.

Fiery Plantain Chips
with Cocomango Dip

Large semi-ripe plantains (or bananas), peeled	2	2
Cooking oil	30 mL	2 tbsp.
Chilli oil	15 mL	1 tbsp.
Chilli powder	5 mL	1 tsp.
Cayenne pepper	2 mL	1/2 tsp.
Finely chopped ripe mango	60 mL	1/4 cup
Sour cream	60 mL	1/4 cup
Coconut rum	30 mL	2 tbsp.
Medium unsweetened coconut, toasted (see How To, page 178)	30 mL	2 tbsp.
Granulated sugar	7 mL	1 1/2 tsp.
Lime juice	7 mL	1 1/2 tsp.
Ground allspice	0.5 mL	1/8 tsp.
Ground nutmeg, just a pinch		

Cut plantain at a sharp angle into 3 mm (1/8 inch) thick slices. Combine next 4 ingredients. Add plantain and toss gently until coated. Arrange in a single layer on 2 parchment paper-lined baking trays. Bake in a 175°C (350°F) oven for 35 to 40 minutes, turning at halftime, until browned around edges. Let stand for 10 minutes.

Combine remaining 8 ingredients. Serve with chips. Serves 6.

1 serving: 695 Kilojoules (166 Calories); 8.0 g Total Fat (3.8 g Mono, 1.2 g Poly, 2.6 g Sat); 4 mg Cholesterol; 22 g Carbohydrate; 2 g Fibre; 1 g Protein; 11 mg Sodium

---

GARNISH
Fresh mango slices

ABOUT PLANTAINS
Plantains can usually be used at any sign of ripeness, but for this recipe you'll want to choose ones that are light yellow with a few black spots and no soft areas. Although they look like bananas, they are nowhere near as easy to peel. To peel, cut off the ends and run a sharp knife through the peel and down the inside curve. Do this three or four more times around the rest of the plantain. The strips should then peel away quite easily.

There are few finer **delights** than introducing your friends to a new taste **experience** – such as chilli-infused plantains **tempered** with a cool and **soothing** coconut and mango dip.

Walnut Ginger Crisps

Plain flour	250 mL	1 cup
Minced crystallised ginger	75 mL	1/3 cup
Ground cardamom	2 mL	1/2 tsp.
Egg whites (large), room temperature (see Tip, below)	3	3
Brown sugar	75 mL	1/3 cup
Walnut halves	300 mL	1 1/4 cups

Combine first 3 ingredients.

Beat egg whites and brown sugar until stiff peaks form. Fold in flour mixture until no dry flour remains.

Fold in walnuts and spread evenly in a greased 22 x 12.5 x 7.5 cm (9 x 5 x 3 inch) loaf pan, lined with parchment paper. Bake in a 175°C (350°F) oven for about 25 minutes until golden and firm. Transfer pan to a wire rack and let stand for 45 minutes. Remove the loaf from pan. Using a serrated knife, cut into 3 mm (1/8 inch) thick slices and arrange on a baking tray. Bake in a 150°C (300°F) oven for about 15 minutes, turning at halftime, until dry and crisp. Transfer baking tray to a wire rack and let stand until cool. Makes about 36 crisps.

1 crisp: 209 Kilojoules (50 Calories); 2.3 g Total Fat (0.3 g Mono, 1.6 g Poly, 0.2 g Sat); 0 mg Cholesterol; 7 g Carbohydrate; trace Fibre; 1 g Protein; 7 mg Sodium

TIP
It is easiest to separate your eggs when they are cold, but always beat them at room temperature.

EXPERIMENT!
To add a delectable touch of sweetness, dip one end of each crisp in melted white chocolate.

Romance the **tantalising** and **aromatic qualities** of cardamom and ginger in these refined crisps that are **well-suited** to serving with a **cheese** tray, custard, **mousse** or ice cream.

Halibut Bites
in Peppered Panko Crust

Plain flour	50 mL	3 tbsp.
Seasoned salt	2 mL	1/2 tsp.
Large egg	1	1
Lemon juice	15 mL	1 tbsp.
Panko breadcrumbs	250 mL	1 cup
Coarsely ground pepper	15 mL	1 tbsp.
Halibut (or other lean, firm fish) fillets (any small bones removed), cut into 2.5 cm (1 inch) pieces	340 g	3/4 lb.
Cooking oil	750 mL	3 cups
Coarse sea salt	5 mL	1 tsp.
Grated lemon zest	5 mL	1 tsp.

Combine flour and seasoned salt in a large resealable freezer bag.

Beat egg and lemon juice in a small shallow bowl.

Combine panko crumbs and pepper in a separate large resealable freezer bag.

Toss halibut in flour mixture until coated. Dip into egg mixture, then toss in crumb mixture until coated.

Heat cooking oil in a large frying pan on medium (see How To, page 106). Shallow-fry halibut for about 2 minutes, turning once, until golden. Transfer with a slotted spoon to a paper towel-lined plate to drain.

Sprinkle with sea salt and lemon zest. Makes about 24 bites.

1 bite: 251 Kilojoules (60 Calories); 3.6 g Total Fat (2.0 g Mono, 1.0 g Poly, 0.3 g Sat); 12 mg Cholesterol; 3 g Carbohydrate; trace Fibre; 4 g Protein; 133 mg Sodium

---

GARNISH
Lemon wedges

ABOUT PANKO
Panko is Japanese cuisine's version of the breadcrumb. Unlike other types of breadcrumbs, panko tends to be flaky-looking. Panko comes in two forms, white and tan. White panko is derived from using crustless bread, while tan panko contains all parts of the bread. If it's unavailable at your local grocer's, you should be able to find it at a specialty food store. For a subtle change to your other dishes, substitute panko where you would usually use regular breadcrumbs.

A welcome, yet unexpected offering at any **gathering**, these cubes of **pure-white halibut** are encased in a **peppery, crisp** golden crust. Your guests will **delight** in their **uniqueness**.

Prawn Corn Cakes
with Lime Sauce

Large egg	1	1
Chopped cooked prawns (peeled and deveined)	250 mL	1 cup
Finely chopped corn kernels	125 mL	1/2 cup
Plain flour	30 mL	2 tbsp.
Chopped fresh coriander	30 mL	2 tbsp.
Yellow polenta	30 mL	2 tbsp.
Sour cream	15 mL	1 tbsp.
Seasoned salt	2 mL	1/2 tsp.
Butter	30 mL	2 tbsp.
Lime juice	10 mL	2 tsp.
Minced jalapeño chillies and smoky barbecue sauce (see Tip, page 172)	7 mL	1 1/2 tsp.

Whisk egg until frothy. Stir in next 7 ingredients to form a thick batter.

Melt about 15 mL (1 tbsp.) butter in a large frying pan on medium. Drop 15 mL (1 tbsp.) portions of batter into pan. Cook for 1 to 2 minutes per side until golden. Transfer cakes to a serving platter and keep warm in a 95°C (200°F) oven. Repeat with remaining batter, adding butter between batches to prevent sticking.

Combine lime juice and jalapeño chillies. Drizzle over corn cakes and serve immediately. Makes about 12 corn cakes.

1 corn cake: 251 Kilojoules (60 Calories); 2.8 g Total Fat (0.8 g Mono, 0.3 g Poly, 1.5 g Sat); 58 mg Cholesterol; 4 g Carbohydrate; trace Fibre; 5 g Protein; 123 mg Sodium

HOW TO PIT AND SLICE AN AVOCADO

GARNISH
Avocado slices
Sour cream

Ever-popular **southwestern flavours** add a contemporary and **appetising** twist. These **refreshing** and **delicious** cakes are best served with **margaritas**, beer or tequila.

Fresh. No matter what delicate morsel is artfully placed upon that verdant bed of lettuce, that single leaf of endive, that perfectly grilled asparagus, you know you're going to experience something crisp, clean and refreshing. But that's only one element in this gourmet interaction. How will the greens be contrasted, complemented or enhanced? Explore, and let your taste buds come alive.

On The Green

Glorious ways with leafy and vegetable greens

Almond Brie Croutons
on Apple-dressed Spinach

Large egg, fork-beaten	1	1
Maple syrup	15 mL	1 tbsp.
Brie cheese round, cut into 6 wedges (see Tip, below)	200 g	7 1/2 oz.
Plain flour	60 mL	1/4 cup
Finely chopped sliced natural almonds	250 mL	1 cup
Maple syrup	30 mL	2 tbsp.
Olive oil	30 mL	2 tbsp.
White balsamic (or wine) vinegar	30 mL	2 tbsp.
Fresh spinach leaves, lightly packed	375 mL	1 1/2 cups
Unpeeled green apple, core removed and cut crosswise into thin rings	1	1

Combine egg and first amount of maple syrup.

Press cheese wedges into flour until coated. Dip into egg mixture, then press firmly into almonds until coated. Freeze for 45 minutes. Place wedges on a baking tray. Bake in a 230°C (450°F) oven for about 7 minutes until almonds start to brown on edges and cheese starts to soften.

Combine next 3 ingredients in a bowl. Add spinach and apple and toss until coated. Spoon onto a serving plate, placing some of the apple rings over spinach. Arrange cheese wedges over top. Serves 6.

1 serving: 1503 Kilojoules (359 Calories); 27.2 g Total Fat (14.2 g Mono, 3.7 g Poly, 8.0 g Sat); 66 mg Cholesterol; 17 g Carbohydrate; 3 g Fibre; 14 g Protein; 248 mg Sodium

TIP
When working with softer cheeses like Brie, you can freeze them for 15 to 20 minutes to make cutting and portioning easier.

This **delicately** dressed spinach salad is **adorned** with decadent 'croutons' – crusted in **almonds** and featuring a soft Brie centre. This **divine delicacy** embodies the word 'heavenly'.

Smoked Tuna and Wasabi Cream
in Endive Boats

Paper-thin English cucumber slices (with peel)	36	36
Rice vinegar	15 mL	1 tbsp.
Granulated sugar	10 mL	1 tsp.
Salt	1 mL	1/4 tsp.
Sour cream	30 mL	2 tbsp.
Grated lime zest	6 mL	1 1/4 tsp.
Wasabi paste	4 mL	3/4 tsp.
Medium Belgian endive (or chicory) leaves	12	12
Can of smoked light tuna slices, drained	120 g	4 1/2 oz.

Combine first 4 ingredients. Let stand for 10 minutes.

Combine next 3 ingredients.

Arrange endive on a serving plate. Arrange 3 overlapping cucumber slices on 1 end of each leaf. Top with a half slice of tuna. Spoon wasabi mixture over top. Makes 12 endive boats.

1 endive boat: 79 Kilojoules (19 Calories); 0.6 g Total Fat (0.1 g Mono, 0.1 g Poly, 0.3 g Sat); 1 mg Cholesterol; 3 g Carbohydrate; 2 g Fibre; 1 g Protein; 60 mg Sodium

---

GARNISH
Salmon caviar

ABOUT SALMON CAVIAR
If you are worried about depleting fish resources, ease your mind. Salmon roe is a non-traditional type of caviar that comes from sustainable sources. Using it will leave the traditional sturgeon sources protected. As another alternative, tiny red caviar will provide a less assertive fish taste but will still maintain a nice, salty flavour.

Seared Scallops Verde

Lime juice	50 mL	3 tbsp.
Olive oil	30 mL	2 tbsp.
Salt	0.5 mL	1/8 tsp.
Pepper	0.5 mL	1/8 tsp.
Large sea scallops	8	8
Chilli powder, sprinkle		
Olive oil	15 mL	1 tbsp.
Tomatillo salsa or salsa verde (green chilli sauce)	125 mL	1/2 cup
Small seedless watermelon triangles, about 12 mm (1/2 inch) thick	8	8

Combine first 4 ingredients. Add scallops and stir. Marinate for 15 minutes. Drain, discarding marinade.

Sprinkle chilli powder over scallops. Heat second amount of olive oil in a frying pan on medium-high. Add scallops and sear for about 1 minute per side until scallops are just opaque.

Spoon small portions of salsa onto 8 small plates. Place watermelon triangles over salsa. Place scallops over watermelon and top with remaining salsa. Serves 8.

1 serving: 293 Kilojoules (70 Calories); 3.6 g Total Fat (2.5 g Mono, 0.4 g Poly, 0.5 g Sat); 5 mg Cholesterol; 7 g Carbohydrate; trace Fibre; 3 g Protein; 102 mg Sodium

---

ABOUT SCALLOPS
Scallops range in colour from beige to creamy pink and should have a seawater smell to them. If scallops are white and odourless, they have most likely been soaked in a solution that plumps them up and increases their longevity. Scallops are notoriously easy to overcook, so it is very important to precisely follow recipe cooking times.

ABOUT SEARING
Searing is the process of cooking at a high temperature to give food an attractive crust. In this recipe you want to achieve the brown crust while cooking the scallops only long enough to lose their shiny, translucent appearance.

An **unpredicted** pairing of **succulent** chilli-crusted **scallops** with the **tang** of a tomatillo salsa is made even more **momentous** with the addition of **fresh** watermelon.

Warm Ginger Chicken
over Spinach

Dry sherry	15 mL	1 tbsp.
Soy sauce	15 mL	1 tbsp.
Sesame oil	5 mL	1 tsp.
Boneless, skinless chicken breast halves, cut into thin strips	225 g	1/2 lb.
Cooking oil	5 mL	1 tsp.
Thinly sliced fresh shiitake mushrooms, stems removed	250 mL	1 cup
Thinly sliced red capsicum (bell pepper)	125 mL	1/2 cup
Finely grated fresh ginger	15 mL	1 tbsp.
Rice vinegar	50 mL	3 tbsp.
Cooking oil	30 mL	2 tbsp.
Sesame oil	15 mL	1 tbsp.
Soy sauce	15 mL	1 tbsp.
Baby spinach leaves, lightly packed	1 L	4 cups

Combine first 3 ingredients. Add chicken and stir. Let stand for 15 minutes.

Heat cooking oil in a frying pan on medium-high. Add chicken mixture and stir-fry for about 5 minutes until no longer pink. Transfer to a bowl.

Add next 3 ingredients to the same frying pan and stir-fry until mushrooms start to soften.

Stir in next 4 ingredients and chicken. Remove from heat and let stand for 5 minutes.

Arrange spinach on a serving plate. Spoon chicken mixture over top, drizzling with pan juices. Serve immediately (see Tip, below). Serves 4.

1 serving: 833 Kilojoules (199 Calories); 13.6 g Total Fat (6.7 g Mono, 4.5 g Poly, 1.5 g Sat); 33 mg Cholesterol; 4 g Carbohydrate; 2 g Fibre; 15 g Protein; 455 mg Sodium

---

GARNISH
Toasted sesame seeds

TIP
It is important that this salad be served immediately to prevent the spinach from becoming limp or wilted.

Sweet Asian flavours **accent** this **delicate**, miniature stir-fry set atop a **verdant**, leafy bed. Set the scene by serving this dish with **soothing jasmine tea** or warm sake.

Praline Pecans, Beetroot and Blue Cheese
on Baby Greens

Medium fresh beetroot, scrubbed clean	1	1
Butter	10 mL	2 tsp.
Brown sugar	60 mL	1/4 cup
Pecan halves	175 mL	3/4 cup
Orange juice	60 mL	1/4 cup
Chopped fresh chives	30 mL	2 tbsp.
Olive oil	30 mL	2 tbsp.
White wine vinegar	30 mL	2 tbsp.
Dijon mustard	15 mL	1 tbsp.
Pepper	0.5 mL	1/8 tsp.
Mixed baby greens, lightly packed	375 mL	1 1/2 cups
Crumbled blue (or goat) cheese	125 mL	1/2 cup

Microwave beetroot, covered, for about 4 minutes until tender. Let stand until cool. Peel and cut into 6 mm (1/4 inch) wedges (see Tip, below).

Heat and stir butter and brown sugar in a frying pan until sugar is dissolved. Stir in pecans. Spread on a baking tray lined with greased foil. Bake in a 190°C (375°F) oven for about 8 minutes, stirring once, until browned. Transfer to cutting board. Let stand until cool, then chop.

Whisk next 6 ingredients together.

Arrange greens in the centre of a serving plate. Arrange beetroot wedges around greens. Sprinkle with cheese and pecans and drizzle with dressing. Serves 4.

1 serving: 1465 Kilojoules (350 Calories); 28.6 g Total Fat (14.5 g Mono, 5.4 g Poly, 6.0 g Sat); 18 mg Cholesterol; 21 g Carbohydrate; 3 g Fibre; 6 g Protein; 279 mg Sodium

TIP
It is advisable to wear gloves when cutting fresh beetroot to avoid staining your hands. It is also easier to peel beetroot after they have been microwaved or roasted – the skins will slip off quite easily.

ALTERNATIVE METHOD
Instead of microwaving your beetroot, you can roast it in the oven. Wrap the beetroot in foil and bake in a 190°C (375°F) oven for about 1 1/2 hours until tender. Remove and discard the foil and let the beetroot cool before peeling.

Vivid **beetroot** and candied pecans add a **distinguished essence** to blue cheese and **mixed greens**. With the addition of a citrus and Dijon dressing, the result is a virtual **kaleidoscope** of flavours.

Miso-glazed Cod
on Ginger-spiked Cucumbers

Paper-thin sliced English cucumber (with peel)	500 mL	2 cups
Paper-thin red onion slice, halved and separated	1	1
Brown sugar	30 mL	2 tbsp.
Mirin	30 mL	2 tbsp.
Rice vinegar	30 mL	2 tbsp.
Finely grated fresh ginger	5 mL	1 tsp.
Black sesame seeds	5 mL	1 tsp.
Sesame seeds	5 mL	1 tsp.
Cod fillets, any small bones removed (about 170 g, 6 oz., each)	2	2
Brown sugar	50 mL	3 tbsp.
Mirin	50 mL	3 tbsp.
White miso	30 mL	2 tbsp.

Combine first 6 ingredients and marinate in refrigerator for 1 hour. Drain, discarding marinade. Arrange on a serving plate.

Sprinkle with sesame seeds.

Place cod fillets on a baking tray. Microwave next 3 ingredients until brown sugar is dissolved and brush over fillets. Grill for 5 to 10 minutes until fish flakes easily when tested with a fork. Serve over cucumbers. Serves 4.

1 serving: 875 Kilojoules (209 Calories); 1.8 g Total Fat (0.5 g Mono, 0.8 g Poly, 0.3 g Sat); 47 mg Cholesterol; 23 g Carbohydrate; 1 g Fibre; 21 g Protein; 301 mg Sodium

---

ABOUT MISO
Miso is a fermented soybean paste that is used in Japanese cooking. There are many varieties of miso with numerous colours and tastes, but two popular varieties are white and red miso. White miso is actually yellowish in colour and has a sweet taste. Red miso is dark brown in colour and imparts a salty flavour. If not available from your grocer, it can be found at an Asian market.

ABOUT MIRIN
Mirin is a sweet Japanese cooking wine with a golden hue. If unavailable at your supermarket, try a specialty food store.

Caramel-coloured glazed cod is set atop an Asian cucumber salad. The outcome is stylishly fresh and stimulating.

Salmon
with Herb Sabayon

Egg yolks (large)	4	4
Dry white wine	75 mL	1/3 cup
Lemon juice	30 mL	2 tbsp.
Granulated sugar	15 mL	1 tbsp.
Chopped fresh basil	15 mL	1 tbsp.
Chopped fresh oregano	15 mL	1 tbsp.
Chopped fresh thyme	5 mL	1 tsp.
Salmon fillet, skin removed	225 g	1/2 lb.
Olive oil	2 mL	1/2 tsp.
Salt, just a pinch		
Pepper, just a pinch		
Butter lettuce leaves	4	4

To make sabayon, whisk first 4 ingredients in a medium stainless steel bowl until frothy. Set over simmering water in a large saucepan so that the bottom of the bowl is not touching the water. Whisk for 1 to 2 minutes until mixture is thickened enough to leave a path on the back of a spoon when you run your finger through it (see How To, below).

Stir in next 3 ingredients.

Place salmon on a greased baking tray. Drizzle with olive oil and sprinkle with salt and pepper. Grill for about 5 minutes until fish flakes easily when tested with a fork. Let stand for 2 minutes.

Arrange salmon over lettuce leaves on a serving plate. Serve with sabayon. Serves 4.

1 serving: 816 Kilojoules (195 Calories); 11.6 g Total Fat (5.1 g Mono, 2.0 g Poly, 3.1 g Sat); 227 mg Cholesterol; 4 g Carbohydrate; trace Fibre; 14 g Protein; 35 mg Sodium

HOW TO PLACE THE BOWL AND CHECK FOR THICKNESS

GARNISH
Lemon peel

Subtle wine essence, **aromatic** lemon and **delicate herb** notes surround a succulent piece of grilled salmon – this small plate is **exquisite** whether served **hot** or **cold**.

Chilli Squid
on Garlic Peas

Squid tubes (about 4 inches, 10 cm, each)	6	6
Soy sauce	15 mL	1 tbsp.
Dried crushed chillies	2 mL	1/2 tsp.
Cooking oil	10 mL	2 tsp.
Thinly sliced red capsicum (bell pepper)	250 mL	1 cup
Sugar snap peas	225 g	1/2 lb.
Garlic cloves, minced	2	2
Sweet chilli sauce	75 mL	1/3 cup
Chilli paste (sambal oelek)	1 mL	1/4 tsp.
Seasoned salt	2 mL	1/2 tsp.
Cooking oil	10 mL	2 tsp.

Cut squid tubes lengthwise to open flat. Score inside surface in a crosshatch pattern. Cut each piece in half and transfer to a bowl. Add soy sauce and chillies and stir. Chill, covered, for 30 minutes.

Heat a frying pan on medium-high until very hot. Add cooking oil. Add next 3 ingredients and stir-fry for about 1 minute until fragrant.

Add next 3 ingredients and stir-fry for about 2 minutes until vegetables are tender but crisp. Transfer to a serving plate.

Add second amount of cooking oil to the same frying pan. Add squid mixture and stir-fry for about 1 minute until squid curls. Arrange over vegetables, drizzling with pan juices. Serves 4.

1 serving: 598 Kilojoules (143 Calories); 5.1 g Total Fat (2.7 g Mono, 1.6 g Poly, 0.5 g Sat); 66 mg Cholesterol; 17 g Carbohydrate; 2 g Fibre; 7 g Protein; 591 mg Sodium

TIP
Like most seafood, squid can become unpalatable when overcooked. Follow the cooking instructions precisely.

One of the **joys of cooking** is boldly stepping into new culinary **territory**. Buying and preparing an unfamiliar ingredient sends **delightful shivers** down the spine. Easily managed, this spicy squid delivers **beautiful results**.

Herb Olive Feta Mélange
over Grilled Asparagus

Ingredient	Metric	Imperial
Fresh asparagus, trimmed of tough ends	454 g	1 lb.
Olive oil	15 mL	1 tbsp.
Salt, sprinkle		
Pepper, sprinkle		
Diced feta cheese	75 mL	1/3 cup
Large pitted green olives	75 mL	1/3 cup
Large pitted kalamata olives	75 mL	1/3 cup
Chopped fresh basil	15 mL	1 tbsp.
Chopped fresh oregano	15 mL	1 tbsp.
Chopped fresh rosemary	5 mL	1 tsp.
Roasted garlic olive oil	30 mL	2 tbsp.

Toss asparagus in olive oil and sprinkle with salt and pepper. Cook on a greased grill pan on medium for about 5 minutes, turning occasionally, until browned. Arrange on a serving platter.

Sprinkle with next 6 ingredients. Drizzle with garlic olive oil. Serves 6.

1 serving: 552 Kilojoules (132 Calories); 11.5 g Total Fat (7.5 g Mono, 1.5 g Poly, 2.4 g Sat); 8 mg Cholesterol; 5 g Carbohydrate; 2 g Fibre; 3 g Protein; 377 mg Sodium

---

GARNISH
Lemon peel
Freshly ground black pepper

HOW TO PIT OLIVES
Although there are olive pitters on the market, pitting by hand is easy. First, you must break the skin so it releases the pit. Do this by rolling and squeezing the olive between your fingers. Or you can press down on the olive with a broad-bladed knife. Once the skin is broken, you should easily be able to remove the pit with your fingers or tweezers.

ALTERNATIVE METHOD
Let the olives and cheese marinate in the herbs and olive oil overnight – this will allow the herb flavours to diffuse throughout the mixture.

A topping of **herbs, olives and feta** provides a **complex** contrast to the simple, fresh **flavour** of grilled asparagus.

Caramel Pork Tenderloin
on Bok Choy

Water	250 mL	1 cup
Granulated sugar	150 mL	2/3 cup
Soy sauce	100 mL	6 tbsp.
Thai hot chillies (or bird's eye chillies), finely chopped (see Tip, below)	3	3
Pork tenderloin, trimmed of fat	340 g	3/4 lb.
Sesame oil	5 mL	1 tsp.
Seasoned salt	1 mL	1/4 tsp.
Baby bok choy, cut in half	500 mL	2 cups

Heat and stir water and sugar in a small saucepan on medium until sugar is dissolved. Boil gently for about 12 minutes, brushing side of pan with a wet pastry brush (see How To, below), until a medium brown colour. Stir in soy sauce and chillies.

Place pork on a greased wire rack set in a foil-lined baking tray. Brush with sesame oil and sprinkle with salt. Bake in a 240°C (475°F) oven for 20 minutes. Brush with 30 mL (2 tbsp.) caramel mixture. Grill for about 2 minutes until internal temperature of pork reaches 70°C (160°F) or desired doneness. Cover with foil and let stand for 10 minutes. Cut into 6 mm (1/4 inch) thick slices.

Cook bok choy in boiling water for about 1 minute until slightly wilted. Drain. Rinse with cold water. Drain well. Serve with pork and remaining caramel mixture. Serves 6.

1 serving: 745 Kilojoules (178 Calories); 2.7 g Total Fat (0.8 g Mono, 0.2 g Poly, 0.7 g Sat); 34 mg Cholesterol; 27 g Carbohydrate; 1 g Fibre; 13 g Protein; 1417 mg Sodium

HOW TO MAKE CARAMEL SAUCE
Brushing the side of the saucepan with a wet pastry brush helps to dissolve any sugar crystals.

TIP
Chillies contain capsaicin in the seeds and ribs, so removing them will reduce the amount of heat. When handling chillies, avoid touching your eyes. Be sure to wash your hands well afterwards.

Feta and Herb Eggplant (Aubergine) Rolls

Asian eggplants (aubergine), ends trimmed	3	3
Olive oil	30 mL	2 tbsp.
Salt, sprinkle		
Pepper, sprinkle		
Canned roasted whole red capsicums (bell peppers), drained, blotted dry, cut into 4 strips each	3	3
Crumbled feta cheese	125 mL	1/2 cup
Herb and garlic cream cheese	60 mL	1/4 cup
Chopped fresh basil	50 mL	3 tbsp.
Rocket	36	36
Wooden cocktail picks	12	12
Balsamic vinegar	30 mL	2 tbsp.

Cut eggplants lengthwise into 6 slices each, about 6 mm (1/4 inch) thick. Discard outside slices. Brush both sides of slices with olive oil and sprinkle with salt and pepper. Cook on a greased grill pan on medium for about 5 minutes until browned. Let stand until cool.

Place 1 strip of red capsicum on each eggplant slice.

Combine next 3 ingredients and spread over red capsicum. Arrange rocket over top. Roll up eggplant slices to enclose filling, securing with wooden picks. Arrange rolls, seam-side down, on a serving plate.

Brush with vinegar. Serve at room temperature. Makes 12 rolls.

1 roll: 347 Kilojoules (83 Calories); 5.6 g Total Fat (2.0 g Mono, 0.3 g Poly, 2.5 g Sat); 11 mg Cholesterol; 5 g Carbohydrate; 1 g Fibre; 2 g Protein; 222 mg Sodium

HOW TO SALT EGGPLANT (AUBERGINE)
If using an eggplant variety that isn't Asian, you may want to salt it. This reduces its natural bitter flavour and makes it less likely to absorb too much oil. Simply cut the eggplant as directed and generously sprinkle with salt. Set aside for an hour and then thoroughly rinse with water. Squeeze out any excess water and blot until completely dry.

ALTERNATIVE METHOD
If you prefer to forgo the grill, you can bake your eggplant slices in a 190°C (375°F) oven for 15 to 20 minutes until lightly browned.

Alluring. The secret of these small plates is hidden on the inside. Sometimes there's a telltale glimpse – perhaps a familiar hue, just peeking out – the rich green of fresh herbs or the lively orange of mango. Maybe it's the aroma that's sending signals to your brain – the beckoning fragrance of ginger, pesto, curry or parmesan – hinting at an exquisite taste that's at first elusive, then familiar. Whatever it is, you're curious. And discovering what's inside is as simple as taking a bite.

Rolled Up & Tucked In

Tenderly wrapped or filled temptations

With an **exciting** variety of tastes and textures, from **tender pork** to crisp, fresh bok choy with a sweet and **spicy caramel** sauce, this dish is both **surprising** and impressive.

The rich royal purple skin of an Asian eggplant lends an intriguing hue to this sophisticated roll. The fresh flavours with smoky accents and a hint of tang are bound to tantalise.

Curried Chicken Samosa Strudel

Ingredient	Metric	Imperial
Cooking oil	10 mL	2 tsp.
Minced onion	375 mL	1 1/2 cups
Madras curry paste	30 mL	2 tbsp.
Garlic cloves, minced	2	2
Canned chickpeas (garbanzo beans), rinsed and drained, mashed	250 mL	1 cup
Chopped cooked chicken breast	250 mL	1 cup
Frozen peas	125 mL	1/2 cup
Grated carrot	125 mL	1/2 cup
Filo pastry sheets, thawed according to packet directions	8	8
Unsalted butter, melted	60 mL	1/4 cup

Heat cooking oil in a frying pan on medium. Add next 3 ingredients and cook until onion starts to soften. Let stand until cool.

Stir in next 4 ingredients.

Layer 4 sheets of filo pastry, lightly brushing each layer with melted butter. Keep remaining filo covered with a damp towel to prevent drying. Spread half of chicken mixture along bottom of sheet, leaving a 3.8 cm (1 1/2 inch) edge on each side. Fold in sides and roll up from bottom to enclose. Place, seam-side down, on an ungreased baking tray. Brush with butter. Cut several small vents on top to allow steam to escape. Repeat. Bake in a 205°C (400°F) oven for about 20 minutes until golden. With a serrated knife, cut strudels diagonally into 7 slices each. Makes 14 slices.

1 slice: 649 Kilojoules (155 Calories); 6.2 g Total Fat (1.9 g Mono, 0.9 g Poly, 2.6 g Sat); 17 mg Cholesterol; 18 g Carbohydrate; 2 g Fibre; 7 g Protein; 148 mg Sodium

HOW TO ROLL STRUDEL

The crisp, delicate and **flaky texture** of **filo pastry** heightens the sensation of biting into these **mildly spiced** strudels.

Seafood Mango Summer Rolls
with Cool Herbs and Chilli Heat

Rice vermicelli	57 g	2 oz.
Chopped fresh mint	30 mL	2 tbsp.
Lime juice	30 mL	2 tbsp.
Sweet chilli sauce	30 mL	2 tbsp.
Fish sauce	10 mL	2 tsp.
Rice paper rounds (18 cm, 7 inch, diameter)	6	6
Fresh coriander leaves	12	12
Cooked medium prawns (shrimp; peeled and deveined), halved lengthwise	6	6
Mango slices, 3 mm (1/8 inch) thick (see Tip, below)	6	6

Cover vermicelli with boiling water. Let stand until just tender. Drain. Rinse with cold water, draining well. Add next 4 ingredients and toss well.

Place 1 rice paper round in a shallow bowl of hot water until just softened (see How To, below). Place on a clean tea towel. Place 2 coriander leaves in the centre of the rice paper and 2 prawn halves over top. Cover with a mango slice. Spoon about 50 mL (3 tbsp.) vermicelli mixture over top. Fold in sides and roll up tightly from bottom to enclose. Repeat. Serve with sweet chilli sauce. Makes 6 rolls.

1 roll: 435 Kilojoules (104 Calories); 0.2 g Total Fat (trace Mono, trace Poly, 0.1 g Sat); 11 mg Cholesterol; 22 g Carbohydrate; trace Fibre; 3 g Protein; 525 mg Sodium

TIP
If fresh mango isn't available, drained, canned mango can be substituted. The texture will be softer but the overall taste won't be compromised.

HOW TO WORK WITH RICE PAPER
In order to become pliable, rice paper must be softened in water. Thicker rice paper (as used in this recipe) requires hotter water whereas the thinner varieties can be softened in cooler water. If working with hot water, make sure to change it as it cools. Always soften one sheet at a time, quickly and evenly. If the rice paper becomes too soft, it may become sticky and hard to work with.

A touch of **chilli heat** mingles with the cool crispness of **mint** and **coriander** in these rolls that are filled with everything light, cool and **refreshing**.

Rocket Pesto Ravioli
with Browned Butter Pine Nuts

Fresh lasagne sheets (15 x 20 cm, 6 x 8 inches, each)	3	3
Rocket, lightly packed	250 mL	1 cup
Pecan halves, toasted (see How To, page 178)	125 mL	1/2 cup
Basil pesto	75 mL	1/3 cup
Grated Asiago cheese	60 mL	1/4 cup
Butter	60 mL	1/4 cup
Pine nuts	50 mL	3 tbsp.
Chopped fresh parsley	10 mL	2 tsp.
Grated lemon zest	5 mL	1 tsp.

Cook lasagne sheets in boiling salted water for about 5 minutes until softened. Drain. Rinse with cold water, draining well.

In a blender or food processor, process next 3 ingredients until smooth. Stir in cheese. Spread 1/4 of rocket mixture over 1 lasagne sheet in a greased pan. Repeat layers, spreading remaining rocket mixture over top. Cut into 8 rectangles.

Melt butter in a frying pan on medium. Add pine nuts and cook until butter is browned. Drizzle over pasta rectangles. Bake, covered, in a 205°C (400°F) oven for about 15 minutes until heated through. Transfer to a serving plate.

Sprinkle with parsley and lemon zest. Makes 8 ravioli.

1 ravioli: 1050 Kilojoules (251 Calories); 19.4 g Total Fat (5.2 g Mono, 2.6 g Poly, 6 g Sat); 21 mg Cholesterol; 15 g Carbohydrate; 2 g Fibre; 6 g Protein; 164 mg Sodium

ABOUT ROCKET
Rocket, also known as 'arugula' in America and 'rucola' in Italy, is a salad green with a lively peppery zing – in some cases it can be quite hot. Because of its vivid flavour, it is rarely served alone. Often it is mixed with other less-distinctly flavoured greens or is used as an accent piece for milder ingredients. In Italy, it is often served salad-style, with thick shavings of the popular Grana Padano cheese.

This deconstructed, highly captivating version of ravioli eliminates the hard labour yet yields a vision that stimulates the senses. With an inspired combination of flavours, the end result is a revelatory experience.

Mushroom Risotto Balls

Ingredient	Metric	Imperial
Cooking oil	5 mL	1 tsp.
Finely chopped white mushrooms	250 mL	1 cup
Minced onion	125 mL	1/2 cup
Arborio rice	125 mL	1/2 cup
Dry white wine	60 mL	1/4 cup
Hot prepared vegetable stock (broth)	325 mL	1 1/3 cups
Pepper	1 mL	1/4 tsp.
Grated Parmesan cheese	60 mL	1/4 cup
Grated lemon zest	2 mL	1/2 tsp.
Asiago cheese cubes (12 mm 1/2 inch,)	12	12
Plain flour	30 mL	2 tbsp.
Cooking oil	750 mL	3 cups
Creamy tomato pasta sauce, warmed	125 mL	1/2 cup

Heat cooking oil in a saucepan on medium. Add mushrooms and onion and cook until softened. Add rice. Heat and stir for 30 seconds.

Add wine. Cook until wine is almost all evaporated. Stir in hot stock and pepper. Bring to the boil. Simmer, covered, on medium-low for about 15 minutes, without stirring, until rice is tender and liquid is absorbed.

Stir in Parmesan cheese and lemon zest. Spoon 30 mL (2 tbsp.) portions of risotto mixture onto a waxed paper-lined baking tray. Let stand for 5 minutes to cool.

Place 1 Asiago cheese cube on each risotto mound. With wet hands, roll into balls, enclosing cheese. Lightly toss in flour.

Heat cooking oil in a large frying pan on medium-high (see How To, below). Shallow-fry risotto balls for 2 to 3 minutes, turning occasionally, until golden and heated through. Transfer to a paper towel-lined plate. Let stand for 2 minutes.

Drizzle pasta sauce on a serving plate. Arrange risotto balls over sauce. Makes about 12 risotto balls.

1 risotto ball: 439 Kilojoules (105 Calories); 6.9 g Total Fat (1.1 g Mono, 0.5 g Poly, 3.4 g Sat); 16 mg Cholesterol; 5 g Carbohydrate; trace Fibre; 5 g Protein; 300 mg Sodium

---

GARNISH
Sprigs of fresh parsley

HOW TO TEST OIL TEMPERATURE
Keep your fried foods crisp, rather than greasy, with properly heated oil that has reached 170–190°C (350–375°F). The easiest way to test the temperature is to use a deep-fry thermometer. If you don't have a thermometer, try either of the following:

- Insert the tip of a wooden spoon. If the oil around it bubbles, the temperature is right.
- Toss in a small piece of bread. If it sizzles and turns brown within 1 minute, the oil is ready.

Inspired by the Italian taste sensation *arancini* (food with a crisp outside and a soft, cheesy centre), a **delectable treasure** of creamy Asiago is neatly tucked into **tempting**, golden mushroom risotto balls.

Crispy Jerk Chicken Rolls

Cooking oil	5 mL	1 tsp.
Chopped onion	250 mL	1 cup
Grated carrot	250 mL	1 cup
Chopped pickled jalapeño chilli	15 mL	1 tbsp.
Caribbean jerk paste (or other spicy paste or marinade)	6 mL	1 1/4 tsp.
Garlic clove, minced	1	1
Ground allspice	0.5 mL	1/8 tsp.
Chopped cooked chicken	250 mL	1 cup
Plain yoghurt	30 mL	2 tbsp.
Spring roll wrappers (15 cm, 6 inch, square)	8	8
Egg white (large)	1	1
Water	15 mL	1 tbsp.
Cooking oil	750 mL	3 cups

Heat cooking oil in a frying pan on medium. Add next 6 ingredients and cook for about 10 minutes until onion is softened.

Stir in chicken and yoghurt.

Arrange wrappers on work surface. Place about 60 mL (1/4 cup) chicken mixture near bottom right corner. Fold corner up and over filling, folding in sides. Dampen edges with a mixture of egg white and water. Roll to opposite corner and press to seal. Repeat.

Heat cooking oil in a large frying pan on medium-high (see How To, page 106). Shallow-fry 2 or 3 rolls at a time, turning often, until golden. Transfer to a paper towel-lined plate. Makes 8 rolls.

1 roll: 628 Kilojoules (150 Calories); 5.1 g Total Fat (2.6 g Mono, 1.3 g Poly, 0.6 g Sat); 16 mg Cholesterol; 18 g Carbohydrate; 1 g Fibre; 9 g Protein; 227 mg Sodium

GARNISH
Sliced jalapeño

EXPERIMENT!
Design your own jerk seasoning by playing around with varying amounts of the following spices: onion salt or flakes, thyme, cinnamon, cloves, allspice, ginger, garlic and cayenne. When you have achieved the right proportions, store in a resealable plastic bag so it's at the ready. Sprinkle on meat before barbecuing or make a simple dip by adding a small amount to sweet-and-sour sauce.

Indulge your guests with the **crisp, fried** fare that is so enjoyed at get-togethers – just make yours a **cut above** the rest with the Jamaican flair of **spicy jerk** chicken.

Parmesan Cones
with Cannellini Mousse

Grated fresh Parmesan cheese (see Tip, below)	175 mL	3/4 cup
Pepper	1 mL	1/4 tsp.
Canned cannellini beans, rinsed and drained	250 mL	1 cup
Basil pesto	15 mL	1 tbsp.
Lemon juice	10 mL	2 tsp.
Olive oil	10 mL	2 tsp.

Cut two 9 cm (3 1/2 inch) diameter circles from heavy paper. Shape into cones and tape or staple securely. Place a sheet of parchment paper on a baking tray (see Tip, below). Trace two 9 cm (3 1/2 inch) diameter circles, about 7.5 cm (3 inches) apart. Turn paper over. Combine cheese and pepper and spread about 15 mL (1 tbsp.) cheese mixture over each circle. Bake in a 175°C (350°F) oven for about 5 minutes until melted and golden. Let stand for 1 minute. Transfer cheese round to a plate. Immediately place 1 paper cone on cheese and roll around cone. Repeat with second cheese round and cone. Let stand until cool. Wipe parchment paper to remove any crumbs. Repeat.

In a blender or food processor, process remaining 4 ingredients until smooth. Spoon into a small freezer bag with a small piece snipped off 1 corner. Pipe into cones. Serve immediately. Makes about 10 cones.

1 cone: 297 Kilojoules (71 Calories); 4.1 g Total Fat (1.3 g Mono, 0.1 g Poly, 1.7 g Sat); 6 mg Cholesterol; 4 g Carbohydrate; 1 g Fibre; 5 g Protein; 161 mg Sodium

---

GARNISH
Sprigs of fresh basil

TIP
Don't cheat yourself by using powdered Parmesan. Grate the fresh stuff for truly magnificent flavour and perfect results.

TIP
Have two separate baking trays at the ready, each with their own parchment paper with circles drawn on, so you can put the second one in the oven while the first one cools.

Although **reminiscent** of a favourite sweet treat, the eyes will play tricks on the **taste buds** when your guests bite into these rich, **savoury** cones. The interplay of Parmesan, basil and lemon is delightfully **unexpected**.

Seta Antojitos Especial

Olive oil	15 mL	1 tbsp.
Chopped portobello mushrooms	1 L	4 cups
Chopped leek (white part only)	125 mL	1/2 cup
Salt	1 mL	1/4 tsp.
Pepper	1 mL	1/4 tsp.
Madeira (red wine)	30 mL	2 tbsp.
Chopped fresh thyme	7 mL	1 1/2 tsp.
Grated havarti cheese	375 mL	1 1/2 cups
Flour tortillas (22 cm, 9 inch, diameter)	2	2

Heat olive oil in a large frying pan on medium-high. Add next 4 ingredients and cook until mushrooms are browned and liquid is all evaporated.

Add Madeira and thyme and cook until wine is all evaporated. Remove from heat.

Stir in cheese. Spread over tortillas, leaving a 12 mm (1/2 inch) border. Roll up to enclose. Place, seam-side down, on a greased baking tray. Bake in a 205°C (400°F) oven until browned and cheese is melted. Let stand for 2 minutes. Trim ends and cut diagonally into 5 slices each. Makes 10 slices.

1 slice: 833 Kilojoules (199 Calories); 14.4 g Total Fat (1.0 g Mono, 0.1 g Poly, 8.9 g Sat); 30 mg Cholesterol; 7 g Carbohydrate; 1 g Fibre; 7 g Protein; 306 mg Sodium

---

GARNISH
Sprigs of fresh thyme

ABOUT MADEIRA
Madeira hails from the island of the same name and is considered a fortified wine. There are four different kinds of Madeira, each based on the variety of grape used – which should be clearly displayed on the label. Malmsey is considered to be sweetest; Bual is of medium sweetness; Verdelho is medium dry; and Sercial is very dry. Madeira goes well with cheese and is best imbibed as an aperitif or dessert wine. It is traditionally served in a small, thin, port-style glass.

This tortilla wrap **surprises**. Madiera and portobello add a **richness** and **body** that completely **satisfies**.

Smoked Salmon Rice Rolls

Mixed baby greens	250 mL	1 cup
Julienned smoked salmon slices (see How To, page 174)	170 g	6 oz.
Julienned English cucumber (see How To, 174)	125 mL	1/2 cup
Enoki mushrooms	85 g	3 oz.
Grated carrot	75 mL	1/3 cup
Julienned spring onion (see How To, page 174)	60 mL	1/4 cup
Sprigs of fresh dill, stems removed	6	6
Rice paper rounds (22 cm, 9 inch, diameter)	6	6
Black sesame seeds (or toasted white sesame seeds)	5 mL	1 tsp.
Ponzu sauce (see Tip, below)	75 mL	1/3 cup

Divide each of the first 7 ingredients into 6 equal portions.

Place 1 rice paper round in a shallow bowl of hot water until just softened (see How To, page 102). Place on a clean tea towel. Arrange 1 portion of filling along centre of rice paper. Fold in sides and roll up tightly from bottom to enclose. Place, seam-side down, on a serving plate. Repeat.

Sprinkle sesame seeds over rolls. Serve with ponzu sauce. Makes 6 rolls.

1 roll with 12 mL (2 1/2 tsp.) sauce: 1599 Kilojoules (382 Calories); 2.1 g Total Fat (0.7 g Mono, 0.4 g Poly, 0.8 g Sat); 7 mg Cholesterol; 78 g Carbohydrate; 1 g Fibre; 12 g Protein; 1815 mg Sodium

TIP
If you can't find ponzu sauce, simply add a little lemon juice to regular soy sauce.

ABOUT ENOKI MUSHROOMS
Enoki mushrooms have a delicate flavour and an unexpected crunchiness. With tiny caps and long thin stems, they are usually found in the produce section in sealed bundles. They last up to two weeks sealed, but must be used immediately if opened. They can be enjoyed fresh and should only ever be lightly cooked. Overcooking will make them stringy and tough.

Smoked salmon adds extra dimension to this special salad roll. The rich, salty fish and the cool, fresh vegetables are balanced in Zen-like proportion.

Precise. When cooking with sharp sticks, you have to make decisions wisely. Senses will be on overdrive. This is food that will be touched as well as tasted. Take a stab at Pork Souvlaki with Savoury Yoghurt or Leek-wrapped Ginger Scallops with Soy Glaze. But venture carefully. You're creating a very special lineup: flavour…spiked.

Skewered

Clever queues of delectable bites

Dukkah Beef Skewers
with Wine Reduction

Balsamic vinegar	60 mL	1/4 cup
Dry red wine	60 mL	1/4 cup
Honey	60 mL	1/4 cup
Hazelnuts (filberts)	14	14
Sesame seeds	10 mL	2 tsp.
Coriander seed	5 mL	1 tsp.
Cumin seed	5 mL	1 tsp.
Grated Reggiano Parmigiano cheese	30 mL	2 tbsp.
Coarsely ground pepper	1 mL	1/4 tsp.
Olive oil	30 mL	2 tbsp.
Dijon mustard	15 mL	1 tbsp.
Beef strip or top loin steak, cut into 6 mm (1/4 inch) slices	340 g	3/4 lb.
Bamboo skewers (8 inches, 20 cm, each), soaked in water for 10 minutes	16	16

Combine first 3 ingredients in a saucepan. Boil gently on medium for about 7 minutes until reduced by half.

Heat and stir next 4 ingredients in a frying pan on medium until toasted and fragrant. Let stand until cool. Transfer to a blender or food processor and process until coarsely ground.

Combine mixture with cheese and pepper on a plate.

Combine olive oil and mustard. Add beef and stir. Thread onto skewers and press into cheese mixture until coated. Cook on a greased grill pan on medium-high for 1 to 2 minutes per side until meat reaches desired doneness. Drizzle half of wine mixture over top. Serve immediately with remaining wine mixture. Makes 16 skewers.

1 skewer with 2 mL (1/2 tsp.) wine reduction: 410 Kilojoules (98 Calories); 6.0 g Total Fat (3.3 g Mono, 0.5 g Poly, 1.7 g Sat); 14 mg Cholesterol; 5 g Carbohydrate; trace Fibre; 5 g Protein; 40 mg Sodium

---

ABOUT DUKKAH
Dukkah is a traditional Middle Eastern spice mix that lends flavour and texture to even the most basic dishes. Although the ingredients vary from cook to cook, they often include sesame seeds, hazelnuts, pistachios and spices native to the local area.

IMBIBE!
Fruited bubbly wines will complement the sweet glaze and earthy spiciness of the coating.

Aromatic spices, seeds and nuts combine to make an exotic coating with as much texture as taste. Expect an exhilarating eating experience that alludes to Middle Eastern tradition.

Thai Chicken
on Lemongrass Skewers

Lean chicken mince	340 g	3/4 lb.
Fine dry breadcrumbs	150 mL	2/3 cup
Brown sugar	15 mL	1 tbsp.
Chopped fresh coriander	15 mL	1 tbsp.
Minced lemongrass, bulb only (root and stalk removed)	15 mL	1 tbsp.
Thai green curry paste	15 mL	1 tbsp.
Garlic clove, minced	1	1
Stalks of lemongrass, outer layers removed	6	6
Sesame oil	30 mL	2 tbsp.

Combine first 7 ingredients.

Press about 60 mL (1/4 cup) chicken mixture around each lemongrass stalk, about 2.5 cm (1 inch) from thick end. Brush with sesame oil. Cook on a greased grill pan on medium-high for about 15 minutes, turning often, until chicken is no longer pink (see Tip, below). Makes 6 skewers.

1 skewer: 896 Kilojoules (214 Calories); 13.2 g Total Fat (2.1 g Mono, 2.0 g Poly, 0.9 g Sat); 0 mg Cholesterol; 12 g Carbohydrate; trace Fibre; 11 g Protein; 226 mg Sodium

---

GARNISH
Sprigs of fresh coriander

TIP
When grilling the skewers, make sure the lemongrass stalk ends are away from the heat. If the ends are too close to the fire or burner, they will be scorched.

ABOUT LEMONGRASS
Lemongrass contains one of the same essential oils that is found in lemon peel. This oil gives the grass that distinctive lemony aroma and flavour.

Fragrant lemon flavour **permeates** curry-flavoured chicken from the inside out with the help of lemongrass skewers. The novel **presentation** is bound to be a topic of conversation.

Leek-wrapped Ginger Scallops
with Soy Glaze

Soy sauce	125 mL	1/2 cup
Brown sugar	30 mL	2 tbsp.
Large leek (white part only), trimmed to 12.5 cm (5 inches)	1	1
Pickled ginger slices, halved	6	6
Large sea scallops	12	12
Wooden cocktail picks	12	12
Water	125 mL	1/2 cup
Soy sauce	30 mL	2 tbsp.

Combine first amount of soy sauce and brown sugar in a saucepan. Simmer on medium-low for about 5 minutes until reduced to a syrupy consistency.

Remove 12 leaves from centre of leek. Blanch in boiling water for 1 minute to soften. Drain and plunge into ice water for 1 minute. Drain well and blot dry.

Roll 1 ginger piece and 1 scallop in each leaf. Secure with cocktail picks (see How To, below).

Combine water and second amount of soy sauce in a frying pan. Bring to a simmer on medium and add skewers. Cook, covered, for about 4 minutes until scallops are opaque. Transfer to a serving plate using a slotted spoon. Serve with brown sugar mixture. Makes 12 skewers.

1 skewer with 5 mL (1 tsp.) glaze: 125 Kilojoules (30 Calories); 0.1 g Total Fat (trace Mono, trace Poly, trace Sat); 5 mg Cholesterol; 4 g Carbohydrate; trace Fibre; 3 g Protein; 590 mg Sodium

HOW TO ASSEMBLE SCALLOP ROLLS

Whereas bacon-wrapped scallops may be too much of a **good** thing, **leek-wrapped** scallops provide the **perfect** light compromise. The **inclusion** of ginger and a salty-sweet **glaze** finish off this small plate **perfectly**.

Rosemary-spiked Meatballs

Lean lamb mince	225 g	1/2 lb.
Grated Greek aged Myzithra cheese (or Parmesean cheese)	60 mL	1/4 cup
Large egg, fork-beaten	1	1
Sun-dried tomato pesto	10 mL	2 tsp.
Grated lemon zest	5 mL	1 tsp.
Chopped fresh rosemary	5 mL	1 tsp.
Sprigs of fresh rosemary (15 cm, 6 inches, each), see Tip, below	4	4

Combine first 6 ingredients. Roll into 12 balls and place on a baking tray. Bake in a 205°C (400°F) oven for about 12 minutes until internal temperature reaches 70°C (160°F). Let stand until cool enough to handle.

Thread 3 meatballs onto each rosemary sprig. Makes 4 skewers.

1 skewer: 833 Kilojoules (199 Calories); 15.2 g Total Fat (6.0 g Mono, 1.2 g Poly, 6.7 g Sat); 91 mg Cholesterol; 2 g Carbohydrate; trace Fibre; 13 g Protein; 375 mg Sodium

---

GARNISH
Lemon wedges

TIP
When preparing your rosemary skewers, remove all the leaves, except for those on the last two inches of each stem. Use the removed leaves in the recipe.

PRESENTATION INSPIRATION
Serve your lamb skewers on a bed of couscous or bulgur for a more rustic appearance.

IMBIBE!
Your best bet for these skewers is a bold red wine, such as a shiraz, rioja or cabernet.

Rosemary's **heady aroma** permeates the air when its sprigs stand in place of skewers for these **Greek-inspired** lamb meatballs. A tzatziki dip can provide the **perfect** accompaniment.

Mahogany Chicken Waves

Brown sugar	30 mL	2 tbsp.
Chilli powder	15 mL	1 tbsp.
Smoked sweet paprika	15 mL	1 tbsp.
Cocoa, sifted if lumpy	5 mL	1 tsp.
Garlic powder	1 mL	1/4 tsp.
Pepper	1 mL	1/4 tsp.
Boneless, skinless chicken breast halves (113–170 g, 4–6 oz., each), cut lengthwise into 4 strips each	2	2
Bamboo skewers (20 cm, 8 inches, each), soaked in water for 10 minutes	8	8
Olive oil	15 mL	1 tbsp.
Salt	2 mL	1/2 tsp.

Combine first 6 ingredients. Add chicken and stir. Chill, covered, for 1 hour.

Thread chicken onto skewers. Brush with olive oil and sprinkle with salt. Cook on a greased grill pan on medium for about 3 minutes per side until no longer pink inside. Makes 8 skewers.

1 skewer: 448 Kilojoules (107 Calories); 3.0 g Total Fat (1.6 g Mono, 0.5 g Poly, 0.6 g Sat); 39 mg Cholesterol; 4 g Carbohydrate; trace Fibre; 15 g Protein; 195 mg Sodium

---

GARNISH
Lime wedges

ABOUT SMOKED PAPRIKA
Smoked Spanish paprika (or *pimentón*) is a much different product from regular paprika. Made by slowly smoking pimientos over oak, it comes in three varieties: mild and sweet (*dulce*); medium bittersweet (*agridulce*); and hot (*picante*). It is most notably used in chorizo sausage and paella.

A cocoa and **smoked sweet** paprika rub lends a **becoming** mahogany hue to **thin strips** of chicken threaded in waves. The presentation is **memorable**, and so is the **bittersweet** taste.

Chilli-crusted Medallions

Large egg, fork-beaten	1	1
Lean pork mince	225 g	1/2 lb.
Uncooked prawns (shrimp; peeled and deveined), coarsely chopped	170 g	6 oz.
Fine dry breadcrumbs	60 mL	1/4 cup
Cornflour	15 mL	1 tbsp.
Seasoned salt	2 mL	1/2 tsp.
Chilli paste (sambal oelek)	60 mL	1/4 cup
Wooden cocktail skewers	12	12
Plain yoghurt	125 mL	1/2 cup

Combine first 6 ingredients. Shape into twelve 5 cm (2 inch) diameter patties and place on a greased baking tray. Brush with chilli paste. Grill for about 3 minutes until browned. Turn and brush with chilli paste. Grill for about 4 minutes until browned and internal temperature reaches 70°C (160°F). Let stand for 5 minutes.

Insert cocktail skewers and place on a serving plate. Serve with yoghurt. Makes 12 skewers.

1 skewer with 15 mL (1 tbsp.) yoghurt: 389 Kilojoules (93 Calories); 5.4 g Total Fat (2.2 g Mono, 0.6 g Poly, 2.1 g Sat); 52 mg Cholesterol; 3 g Carbohydrate; trace Fibre; 7 g Protein; 226 mg Sodium

---

EXPERIMENT!
Instead of sambal oelek, you can use any type of hot sauce you like. Grocery stores have a mind-boggling number of varieties that differ based on their heat, the type of pepper used and other ingredients, such as roasted capsicum (bell pepper) and garlic. Changing your sauce will subtly change the taste.

Made to be **dipped**, these miniature seafood and pork patties have a **fiery presence** that begs for the relief of **cool yoghurt**. Not for the **faint-hearted**, these small eats should be reserved for your most **flame-proofed** guests.

Sesame Chilli Vegetable Skewers

Red capsicum (bell pepper) pieces, 2.5 cm (1 inch) each	32	32
Peeled jicama (or fresh Jerusalem artichoke) pieces, 2.5 cm (1 inch) wide, 6 mm (1/4 inch) thick	8	8
Small whole white mushrooms	8	8
Onion pieces, 2.5 cm (1 inch) each	8	8
Zucchini (courgette) slices (with peel), 12 mm (1/2 inch) thick	8	8
Bamboo skewers (15 cm, 6 inches, each), soaked in water for 10 minutes	8	8
Sesame oil	75 mL	1/3 cup
Thai chilli (see Tip, page 94), minced	1	1
Finely grated fresh ginger	10 mL	2 tsp.
Granulated sugar	10 mL	2 tsp.
Salt	2 mL	1/2 tsp.

Thread first 5 ingredients onto skewers.

Combine remaining 5 ingredients. Cook skewers on a greased grill pan on medium for 10 to 15 minutes, brushing occasionally with sesame oil mixture, until vegetables are tender but crisp. Brush with sesame oil mixture and transfer to a serving plate. Makes 8 skewers.

1 skewer: 435 Kilojoules (104 Calories); 9.1 g Total Fat (3.5 g Mono, 3.8 g Poly, 1.3 g Sat); 0 mg Cholesterol; 6 g Carbohydrate; 1 g Fibre; 1 g Protein; 149 mg Sodium

PRESENTATION INSPIRATION
The way you cut your vegetables can greatly affect presentation. Crinkle cutters can be used, and even just cutting at a different angle can show you care enough to think about how your food is displayed. But when working with skewers, make sure each vegetable piece is cut roughly the same size to ensure even cooking.

These chilli and ginger-basted vegetable skewers provide a colourful complement to any array of small plates. The crisp pieces of jicama are especially well-suited to the Asian-inspired baste.

Tuna Skewers

Soy sauce	30 mL	2 tbsp.
Sesame oil	30 mL	2 tbsp.
Pepper	2 mL	1/2 tsp.
Tuna steak, cut into 2.5 cm (1 inch) cubes	454 g	1 lb.
Finely chopped pistachios toasted (see How To, page 178)	125 mL	1/2 cup
Bamboo skewers (20 cm, 8 inches, each), soaked in water for 10 minutes	6	6

Combine first 3 ingredients in a large resealable freezer bag. Add tuna and marinate for 30 minutes in refrigerator. Drain, discarding marinade.

Press tuna into pistachios until coated. Thread onto skewers. Cook on a greased grill pan on medium-high for about 1 minute per side until browned. Makes 6 skewers.

1 skewer: 757 Kilojoules (181 Calories); 10.1 g Total Fat (4.5 g Mono, 3.6 g Poly, 1.5 g Sat); 36 mg Cholesterol; 3 g Carbohydrate; 1 g Fibre; 19 g Protein; 292 mg Sodium

ABOUT TUNA
If you are someone who does not enjoy rare meat, fresh tuna is not the dish for you. Tuna is always served rare, or at the most, medium-rare. Tuna will become quite tasteless if it is overcooked.

Perhaps the ultimate in **decadent barbecue** fare, these pistachio-crusted **tuna** skewers are sure to be met with **delighted** exclamations of **approval**.

Pork Souvlaki
with Savoury Yoghurt

Red wine	60 mL	1/4 cup
Olive oil	50 mL	3 tbsp.
Greek seasoning	30 mL	2 tbsp.
Garlic cloves, minced	3	3
Lemon juice	15 mL	1 tbsp.
Pork tenderloin, cut into 2.5 cm (1 inch) pieces	340 g	3/4 lb.
Bamboo skewers (10 cm, 4 inches, each), soaked in water for 10 minutes	6	6
Greek pita breads (18 cm, 7 inch, diameter)	3	3
Plain yoghurt	125 mL	1/2 cup
Chopped roasted red capsicum (bell pepper)	30 mL	2 tbsp.
Greek seasoning	15 mL	1 tbsp.

Combine first 5 ingredients in a medium resealable freezer bag. Add pork and marinate in refrigerator for 2 hours. Drain, discarding marinade (see Tip, below).

Thread pork onto skewers. Cook on a greased grill pan on medium for about 5 minutes per side until meat reaches desired doneness.

Grill pita breads for 1 to 2 minutes per side until heated through. Cut into 6 pieces each. Arrange on a serving plate with pork skewers.

Combine remaining 3 ingredients. Serve with pork skewers and pita. Serves 6.

1 serving: 795 Kilojoules (190 Calories); 6.1 g Total Fat (3.6 g Mono, 0.7 g Poly, 1.3 g Sat); 36 mg Cholesterol; 17 g Carbohydrate; 1 g Fibre; 15 g Protein; 350 mg Sodium

TIP
If you want to baste your skewers with any leftover marinade, it is important it be boiled first. Doing this will prevent any contamination from the raw meat. Never save and reuse uncooked marinade.

PRESENTATION INSPIRATION
For a clever serving vessel for your yoghurt, remove the side (or top) third of a red capsicum (bell pepper). Remove all ribs and seeds, and wash. Then fill the red capsicum with the yoghurt and include a small spoon.

Cooked **traditionally** on skewers, this **simple** Greek fare is elevated to **gourmet** proportions with an accompanying yoghurt dip flavoured with **savoury**, roasted red capsicums (bell peppers) and Mediterranean **seasonings**.

Candied Chicken Sticks

Maple syrup	125 mL	1/2 cup
Chilli garlic sauce	30 mL	2 tbsp.
Indonesian sweet soy sauce (or kecap manis)	30 mL	2 tbsp.
Boneless, skinless chicken breast halves, cut lengthwise into 6 mm (1/4 inch) thick slices	225 g	1/2 lb.
Bamboo skewers (20 cm, 8 inches, each), soaked in water for 10 minutes	8	8
Finely shredded suey choy (Chinese cabbage), lightly packed	500 mL	2 cups
Spring onions, cut into 7.5 cm (3 inch) lengths	2	2
Rice vinegar	15 mL	1 tbsp.

Combine first 3 ingredients. Reserve 60 mL (1/4 cup) syrup mixture. Combine chicken and remaining syrup mixture in a medium resealable freezer bag. Marinate in refrigerator for at least 6 hours or overnight. Drain, discarding marinade.

Thread chicken onto skewers. Cook on a well-greased grill pan on medium for 1 to 2 minutes per side until chicken is glazed and no longer pink inside. Brush with 30 mL (2 tbsp.) reserved syrup mixture.

Toss cabbage and spring onion together on a serving platter.

Stir vinegar into remaining syrup mixture and drizzle over cabbage mixture. Top with skewers. Serves 4.

1 serving: 523 Kilojoules (125 Calories); 4.4 g Total Fat (1.6 g Mono, 1.0 g Poly, 1.2 g Sat); 37 mg Cholesterol; 10 g Carbohydrate; 1 g Fibre; 11 g Protein; 243 mg Sodium

---

GARNISH
Toasted sesame seeds

ABOUT SOAKING SKEWERS
It is important to properly soak the skewers before grilling so they don't burn or, worse yet, catch on fire. The soaking will also prevent them from leaving any dry splinters in the meat.

Maple **syrup** and Indonesian sweet **soy sauce** give these chicken skewers a delicious, yet **intangible, sweetness**. Your guests will find the flavours familiar, yet somehow **exotic and elusive.**

Halvah Ice-cream Sundaes
with Orange Honey Figs

Vanilla halvah, cut into 12 mm (1/2 inch) pieces	125 mL	1/2 cup
Vanilla ice-cream, softened	250 mL	1 cup
Dried figs, chopped	4	4
Orange juice	125 mL	1/2 cup
Honey	50 mL	3 tbsp.
Vanilla sesame snaps (or sesame seed bars), crushed	75 ml	1/3 cup

Freeze halvah for about 10 minutes until very firm. Stir into ice-cream. Freeze for about 1 1/2 hours until firm.

Combine next 3 ingredients in a saucepan. Simmer on medium-low until reduced to a syrupy consistency. Let stand until cool.

Scoop ice-cream mixture onto 4 small plates. Sprinkle about 10 mL (2 tsp.) sesame snaps on 1 side of ice-cream and spoon fig mixture on opposite side. Sprinkle remaining sesame snaps over top. Makes 4 sundaes.

1 sundae: 1641 Kilojoules (392 Calories); 16.0 g Total Fat (trace Mono, 0.1 g Poly, 6.4 g Sat); 60 mg Cholesterol; 57 g Carbohydrate; 3 g Fibre; 7 g Protein; 84 mg Sodium

---

GARNISH
Grated orange zest

ABOUT HALVAH
This Middle Eastern confection is typically made from sesame seeds and honey and occasionally includes chopped dried fruit or pistachio nuts. It's readily available in wrapped bars or long slabs from which individual slices can be cut. Variations of halvah are produced in different regions including Asia and continental Europe. You may also find halvah made from a variety of other ingredients such as sunflower seeds, various nuts, beans, lentils and vegetables, including carrots, pumpkins, yams and squash.

Transport your guests to the Middle East with this sweet combination of halvah, ice cream and syrupy figs. Mysterious and adventurous, it's the perfect blend of texture contrasts.

Crisp Cinnamon Banana Boats

Small bananas, peeled and trimmed to 10 cm (4 inches) each	4	4
Flour tortillas (15 cm, 6 inch, diameter)	4	4
Butter, melted	60 mL	1/4 cup
Granulated sugar	60 mL	1/4 cup
Ground cinnamon	10 mL	2 tsp.
Caramel (or plain) Irish cream liqueur	50 mL	3 tbsp.
Chocolate hazelnut spread	50 mL	3 tbsp.
Caramel (or butterscotch) ice-cream topping	150 mL	2/3 cup

Place 1 banana on each tortilla. Fold in sides and roll up tightly from bottom to enclose. Secure with wooden picks (see How To, below).

Brush with melted butter and roll in a mixture of sugar and cinnamon. Place on a baking tray. Bake in a 230°C (450°F) oven for about 8 minutes until golden. Cut in half diagonally.

Whisk liqueur and chocolate spread together until smooth. Drizzle onto a serving plate. Drizzle with ice-cream topping. Arrange rolls over top. Serves 8.

1 serving: 1268 Kilojoules (303 Calories); 9.5 g Total Fat (2.4 g Mono, 0.6 g Poly, 4.5 g Sat); 15 mg Cholesterol; 52 g Carbohydrate; 2 g Fibre; 3 g Protein; 294 mg Sodium

HOW TO ROLL TORTILLAS

There's something **infatuating** about the combination of bananas and caramel. Maybe it's the **silky smoothness**, maybe the **sweetness**. Whatever the appeal, it's nothing less than **heavenly**.

Cappuccino Meringue Stack

Icing sugar	30 mL	2 tbsp.
Instant coffee granules, crushed to a fine powder	10 mL	2 tsp.
Cornflour	7 mL	1 1/2 tsp.
Skim milk powder	7 mL	1 1/2 tsp.
Ground cinnamon, just a pinch		
Egg whites (large), room temperature	2	2
Brown sugar	30 mL	2 tbsp.
Vanilla extract	2 mL	1/2 tsp.
Semi-sweet chocolate baking square (28 g, 1 oz.), chopped	1	1

Combine first 5 ingredients.

Beat egg whites until soft peaks form. Gradually add brown sugar, beating until stiff peaks form. Fold in vanilla and coffee mixture. Spoon into a large freezer bag with a piece snipped off 1 corner. Pipe onto a parchment paper-lined baking tray in a spiral pattern, leaving a 12 mm (1/2 inch) space between each round (see How To, below). Bake in a 120°C (250°F) oven for 1 1/2 hours. Let stand on baking tray set on a wire rack until cool. Break into pieces and stack on a large plate.

Microwave chocolate on medium (50%) for about 1 minute, stirring every 15 seconds, until almost melted. Stir until smooth. Drizzle over meringue stack. Serves 6.

1 serving: 259 Kilojoules (62 Calories); 1.3 g Total Fat (0 g Mono, 0 g Poly, 0.8 g Sat); trace Cholesterol; 11 g Carbohydrate; trace Fibre; 2 g Protein; 23 mg Sodium

HOW TO PIPE AND BREAK MERINGUE

Melt-in-your-mouth meringue is given a twist with the addition of coffee, chocolate and just a hint of cinnamon. It's light on the palate, but certainly gets top grades for its refined flavour.

Raspberry Crème Brûlée

Ingredient	Metric	Imperial
Seedless raspberry jam	75 mL	1/3 cup
Raspberry liqueur	15 mL	1 tbsp.
Pouring cream	375 mL	1 1/2 cups
White chocolate baking squares (28 g, 1 oz., each), chopped	4	4
Egg yolks (large)	4	4
Granulated sugar	30 mL	2 tbsp.
Raspberry liqueur	15 mL	1 tbsp.
Granulated sugar	60 mL	1/4 cup

Place 4 greased 175 mL (6 oz.) ramekins in a 22 x 22 cm (9 x 9 inch) baking pan. Whisk jam and liqueur together until smooth. Spoon into ramekins and chill for about 30 minutes until firm.

Heat cream in a saucepan on medium until bubbles form around edge of pan. Remove from heat. Add chocolate and stir until melted.

Whisk next 3 ingredients together. Gradually whisk into cream mixture. Carefully pour into ramekins (see How To, below). Pour boiling water into pan until water comes halfway up sides of ramekins. Bake in a 150°C (300°F) oven for about 50 minutes until centres only wobble slightly. Transfer ramekins to a wire rack to cool completely. Chill, covered, for at least 6 hours or overnight.

Sprinkle 15 mL (1 tbsp.) sugar over each. Grill for about 5 minutes until sugar is browned and bubbling. Let stand for 5 minutes before serving. Makes 4 crème brûlées.

1 crème brûlée: 2784 Kilojoules (665 Calories); 46.3 g Total Fat (11.3 g Mono, 1.8 g Poly, 27.0 g Sat); 310 mg Cholesterol; 56 g Carbohydrate; 0 g Fibre; 7 g Protein; 69 mg Sodium

HOW TO POUR CUSTARD INTO RAMEKINS
In order to avoid disturbing the jam layer, carefully pour the custard over the back of a spoon.

GARNISH
Fresh raspberries

There's **treasure** hidden beneath a **crisp**, sugary crust. Dig down to find the velvety splendour of raspberry, **chocolate** and whipping cream. **Simple** preparation, yet this dessert is nothing but **decadent**.

Caramel Rum S'Mores

Large marshmallows	6	6
Caramels	6	6
Pouring cream	60 mL	1/4 cup
Spiced rum	30 mL	2 tbsp.
Vanilla extract	2 mL	1/2 tsp.
Large marshmallows	8	8
Small chocolate brownies	8	8
Cocktail picks or bamboo skewers	8	8

Microwave first 5 ingredients in a deep bowl (see Tip, below) on medium (50%) for about 5 minutes, stirring every 60 seconds, until almost melted. Stir until smooth. Cover to keep warm.

On a baking tray, place 1 marshmallow over each brownie. Grill for about 1 minute until marshmallows are golden.

Push skewers through top of marshmallows and into brownies. Serve with caramel sauce. Makes 8 s'mores.

1 s'more with 15 mL (1 tbsp.) sauce: 770 Kilojoules (184 Calories); 8.0 g Total Fat (0.9 g Mono, 0.4 g Poly, 3.0 g Sat); 19 mg Cholesterol; 26 g Carbohydrate; 1 g Fibre; 2 g Protein; 83 mg Sodium

TIP
Because marshmallows expand when microwaved, be sure to use a large, deep bowl when heating the marshmallows for the caramel sauce. If you prefer, use a double boiler instead and make the sauce on the stovetop.

PRESENTATION INSPIRATION
If you're invited to a campfire or hosting one yourself, why not add a touch of gourmet to the event? Gather some sticks for roasting marshmallows and surprise everyone with your idea. Have the caramel sauce made in advance or purchase some ready-made caramel sauce to use as a dip. Let everyone roast their own marshmallows and provide brownies and skewers so people can create their own special s'mores.

Brownies topped with **ooey, gooey** marshmallows, grilled and served with a **rum caramel sauce** for dipping. Sure to bring back memories of roasting marshmallows over a campfire.

Lavalicious Chocolate Kisses

Bittersweet chocolate baking square (28 g, 1 oz.), chopped	1	1
Semi-sweet chocolate baking square (28 g, 1 oz.), chopped	1	1
Butter	60 mL	1/4 cup
Large eggs	2	2
Icing sugar	150 mL	2/3 cup
Vanilla extract	5 mL	1 tsp.
Plain flour	60 mL	1/4 cup

Heat first 3 ingredients in a saucepan on lowest heat, stirring often, until chocolate is almost melted. Remove from heat. Stir until smooth. Let stand for 10 minutes.

Whisk next 3 ingredients together. Stir in chocolate mixture until combined.

Stir in flour until just moistened. Spoon into a small freezer bag with a small piece snipped off 1 corner. Fill 12 greased 30 mL (1 oz.) ramekins 3/4 full. Bake in a 220°C (425°F) oven for about 6 minutes until edges are set but centres still look wet and wobble slightly. Makes 12 kisses.

1 kiss: 435 Kilojoules (104 Calories); 6.3 g Total Fat (1.3 g Mono, 0.3 g Poly, 3.6 g Sat); 41 mg Cholesterol; 11 g Carbohydrate; trace Fibre; 2 g Protein; 37 mg Sodium

---

GARNISH
Sifted cocoa

ABOUT CHOCOLATE
Officially, there are three kinds of chocolate: dark, milk and white. Dark chocolate contains cocoa liquor, cocoa butter and sugar. The higher the cocoa content, the more bitter the chocolate. Milk chocolate contains the same ingredients as dark chocolate, with the addition of milk powder for a lighter colour with a creamier texture and taste. White chocolate contains milk, sugar and cocoa butter, but no cocoa liquor. That explains the pale, ivory colour of this sweet confection which, by many people's standards, does not fit the definition of chocolate at all.

Decadent little chocolate bites with **molten** centres – this is one kiss you **won't soon forget.**

Pomegranate Jellies

Envelope of unflavoured gelatine (about 15 mL, 1 tbsp.)	7 g	1/4 oz.
Pomegranate juice	250 mL	1 cup
Water	60 mL	1/4 cup
Icewine (or late harvest wine)	60 mL	1/4 cup
Granulated sugar	30 mL	2 tbsp.

Sprinkle gelatine over juice and water in a saucepan. Let stand for 1 minute.

Add icewine and sugar. Heat and stir until sugar is dissolved. Pour into 6 glasses or small dessert cups. Chill for about 3 hours until set. Serves 6.

1 serving: 251 Kilojoules (60 Calories); 0 g Total Fat (0 g Mono, 0 g Poly, 0 g Sat); 0 mg Cholesterol; 13 g Carbohydrate; 0 g Fibre; trace Protein; 10 mg Sodium

---

GARNISH
Fresh mint leaves
Fresh raspberries
Fresh strawberries

ABOUT ICEWINE
Icewine is made by picking overripe grapes that have frozen on the vine on a cold night. The grapes are then pressed before they thaw. Because the water in the grapes is still frozen, the juice is much more concentrated, resulting in an extremely sweet dessert wine. Because the process of making icewine is labour-intensive, the price tends to be quite high.

Definitely not a kid's dessert – this truly grown-up jelly is elevated to gourmet fare with the flavour of pomegranate and the addition of icewine.

Ginger-poached Pears

Small, firm peeled pears	4	4
Water	750 mL	3 cups
Icewine (or late harvest wine)	250 mL	1 cup
Granulated sugar	125 mL	1/2 cup
Lemon juice	30 mL	2 tbsp.
Piece of fresh ginger (2.5 cm, 1 inch, length), chopped	1	1

Core pears from the bottom, leaving stems intact. Cut a thin slice from bottoms so pears will stand upright.

Combine remaining 5 ingredients in a large saucepan. Bring to the boil, stirring to dissolve sugar. Reduce heat to medium-low. Lay pears on their sides in pan. Simmer, covered, for 20 to 25 minutes, turning occasionally, until pears are tender when pierced with a knife. Transfer pears to a serving dish, using a slotted spoon. Remove and discard ginger. Boil poaching liquid on medium-high for about 20 minutes until reduced and slightly thickened. Serve with pears (see How To, below). Serves 4.

1 serving: 904 Kilojoules (216 Calories); 0.2 g Total Fat (trace Mono, trace Poly, trace Sat); 0 mg Cholesterol; 47 g Carbohydrate; 4 g Fibre; 1 g Protein; 2 mg Sodium

HOW TO SLICE PEARS FOR A FLOWER PETAL APPEARANCE
For an attractive presentation, you can cut your pears so that they have a flower shape. Make several cuts around the pear, starting about halfway up and cutting through to the bottom. Cut just to the centre of the pear, where the core has been removed. Once you have made cuts all around the pear, gently spread out to make a flower shape.

GARNISH
Chopped crystallised ginger
Lemon peel

Ultra-sweet icewine is the **perfect** ingredient for **poaching** pears. Paired with ginger and lemon, it's one hot ticket to a **higher level** of taste.

Vanillacotta
with Liqueur

Unflavoured gelatine	20 mL	4 tsp.
Cold water	50 mL	3 tbsp.
Pouring cream	125 mL	1/2 cup
Packet of vanilla sugar	9 g	1/4 oz.
Vanilla flavoured yoghurt (not fat-free)	250 mL	1 cup
Vanilla (or hazelnut) liqueur	125 mL	1/2 cup

Sprinkle gelatine over cold water in a saucepan. Let stand for 1 minute. Add cream and vanilla sugar. Heat and stir until sugar is dissolved. Remove from heat.

Whisk in yoghurt until combined. Pour into 6 small glasses. Chill, covered, for at least 6 hours or overnight.

Pour liqueur over vanillacottas. Serves 6.

1 serving: 745 Kilojoules (178 Calories); 7.3 g Total Fat (2.0 g Mono, 0.3 g Poly, 4.6 g Sat); 28 mg Cholesterol; 18 g Carbohydrate; 0 g Fibre; 2 g Protein; 35 mg Sodium

---

GARNISH
Toasted hazelnuts (filberts)

HOW TO MAKE YOUR OWN VANILLA SUGAR
Vanilla sugar can be used in cakes, jams, cocktails and pretty much anything else that requires a touch of vanilla essence. To make your own vanilla sugar, place a vanilla bean in a jar and cover it with sugar. Use more beans for larger jars of sugar. Let sit for about two weeks before removing the bean. Afterwards, you can save the beans in a separate jar for future use.

When you get something as **sinfully rich** as this, you'll want it to last forever. Vanilla **mingles** with the **slight tang** of yoghurt to provide **perfect** balance.

Lemon Thyme Sorbet

Thin lemon slices	4	4
Water	125 mL	1/2 cup
Granulated sugar	50 mL	3 tbsp.
Sprigs of fresh thyme	2	2
Lemon juice	30 mL	2 tbsp.
Grated lemon zest	2 mL	1/2 tsp.
Finely chopped fresh thyme	2 mL	1/2 tsp.

Press lemon slices into 4 shot glasses and freeze.

Combine next 3 ingredients in a saucepan. Boil gently on medium for about 8 minutes. Remove and discard thyme sprigs.

Stir in remaining 3 ingredients. Let stand until slightly cooled. Pour into prepared shot glasses. Freeze for about 2 hours until firm. Serves 4.

1 serving: 159 Kilojoules (38 Calories); trace Total Fat (0 g Mono, 0 g Poly, 0 g Sat); 0 mg Cholesterol; 10 g Carbohydrate; trace Fibre; trace Protein; trace Sodium

---

GARNISH
Sprigs of fresh thyme

ABOUT SORBET
Sorbet is the perfect palate cleanser because, unlike sherbet and ice-cream, it does not contain any dairy. This leaves it light and refreshing. Although sweet varieties are also popular for dessert, savoury flavours are being used more and more often as palate cleansers.

PRESENTATION INSPIRATION
A palate cleanser is simply meant to refresh the palate – not satiate your guests. A tiny scoop the size of a melon ball will suffice nicely. But how you present it gives you an opportunity to let your imagination soar. It can be served on a small block of ice, in a large wonton spoon or set atop crushed ice in an egg cup – just remember to always include a spoon.

Citrus sorbet makes a great palate cleanser when there are lots of different flavours vying for your taste buds' attention. A sorbet shooter is just enough to refresh the palate between small plates.

Calabrese Bites

Calabrese salami slices, halved (about 57 g, 2 oz.)	6	6
Medium-sized fresh basil leaves	12	12
Cherry tomatoes, halved	6	6
Small bocconcini cheese balls	12	12
Pieces of sun-dried tomato in oil, about 12 mm (1/2 inch) each	12	12
Wooden cocktail picks	12	12
Balsamic vinegar	15 mL	1 tbsp.
Coarsely ground pepper, sprinkle		

Arrange salami on work surface, placing 1 basil leaf over each piece. Place next 3 ingredients in a row over top. Fold up ends of salami and insert a wooden pick from end to end to secure (see How To, below). Place on a baking tray.

Drizzle with balsamic vinegar. Bake in a 205°C (400°F) oven for about 3 minutes until hot. Sprinkle with pepper and serve immediately. Makes 12 bites.

1 bite: 397 Kilojoules (95 Calories); 7.8 g Total Fat (0.3 g Mono, 0.1 g Poly, 2.7 g Sat); 16 mg Cholesterol; 1 g Carbohydrate; trace Fibre; 6 g Protein; 74 mg Sodium

HOW TO ASSEMBLE BITES

ALTERNATIVE METHOD
Instead of baking these bites, simply microwave on high for 15 to 20 seconds until hot.

GARNISH
Sprigs of fresh basil

Evocative of a sunny Italian countryside picnic, these **exceptional** salami and **bocconcini** bites combine many of the fresh flavours so characteristic of Tuscany.

Braised Hoisin Spareribs

Sweet-and-sour-cut pork ribs (breastbone removed)	680 g	1 1/2 lbs.
Hoisin sauce	60 mL	1/4 cup
Sweet chilli sauce	60 mL	1/4 cup
Sesame oil	30 mL	2 tbsp.
Soy sauce	30 mL	2 tbsp.
Water	30 mL	2 tbsp.
Garlic cloves, minced	2	2
Chinese five-spice powder	5 mL	1 tsp.

Place ribs, bone-side down, in a baking pan.

Stir remaining 7 ingredients until smooth. Pour 150 mL (2/3 cup) of sauce mixture over ribs. Bake, covered, in a 175°C (350°F) oven for 30 minutes. Bake, uncovered, for about 45 minutes, basting with pan juices and remaining sauce mixture, until fully cooked and tender. Cover with foil and let stand for 10 minutes. Transfer to cutting board and cut ribs into 1-bone portions. Makes about 12 ribs.

1 rib: 850 Kilojoules (203 Calories); 15.8 g Total Fat (6.7 g Mono, 2.2 g Poly, 5.4 g Sat); 44 mg Cholesterol; 5 g Carbohydrate; trace Fibre; 10 g Protein; 420 mg Sodium

---

GARNISH
Sliced spring onion

ABOUT SWEET-AND-SOUR-CUT RIBS
Sweet-and-sour-cut ribs are simply spareribs (also known as side ribs) cut into five-centimetre portions. If you cannot easily find this cut, your local butcher will be glad to prepare it for you.

PRESENTATION INSPIRATION
The presentation of your food can be greatly improved simply by varying your cutting. In this recipe, consider cutting the spring onion garnish on a sharp angle. It's easy and adds a special touch.

Hoisin and five-spice powder lend an **aromatic** Asian influence to these **small morsels** with a lively **chilli heat.** Serve with finger bowls so your guests can engage in a more refined eating **experience.**

Prosciutto-wrapped Bread Sticks
with Cantaloupe Purée

Coarsely chopped ripe cantaloupe	250 mL	1 cup
Ground cinnamon, just a pinch		
Thin slices of prosciutto ham (about 113 g, 4 oz.)	8	8
Bread sticks (15–20 cm, 6–8 inches, each)	8	8

In a blender or food processor, process cantaloupe and cinnamon until smooth. Pour into 8 small glasses.

Wrap 1 slice of prosciutto around 1 end of each bread stick. Place 1 bread stick across rim of each glass. Serve immediately. Serves 8.

1 serving: 326 Kilojoules (78 Calories); 2.5 g Total Fat (0.4 g Mono, 0.4 g Poly, 0.7 g Sat); 11 mg Cholesterol; 9 g Carbohydrate; trace Fibre; 5 g Protein; 444 mg Sodium

---

ABOUT CANTALOUPE
Although a cantaloupe's colour and texture will change after being picked, all its flavour comes from being allowed to properly ripen on the vine – so it is important to choose a ripe one. It should have a slightly musky odour because an odourless melon will lack flavour. Push on the melon's base, opposite the stem. It should give a little without being too soft. Soft and lumpy melons are past their prime and will be quite watery.

EXPERIMENT!
Try using seasoned bread sticks to vary the flavour. If they are too long, simply cut them in half before serving.

This modernised version of classic proscuitto-wrapped melon perfectly balances the salty ham with the invigorating sweetness of the cantaloupe purée. The varied textures also add a sensual dimension to the flavour experience.

Strawberry Salsa
with Goat Cheese and Melba Toast

Finely chopped fresh strawberries	500 mL	2 cups
White balsamic vinegar	30 mL	2 tbsp.
Minced fresh basil	25 mL	1 1/2 tbsp.
Minced fresh chives	7 mL	1 1/2 tsp.
Granulated sugar	5 mL	1 tsp.
Coarsely ground pepper	2 mL	1/2 tsp.
Soft goat (chèvre) cheese	60 mL	1/4 cup
Round Melba toasts	24	24

Combine first 6 ingredients. Let stand for 30 minutes to blend flavours.

Serve cheese with Melba toast and strawberry mixture. Serves 8.

1 serving: 372 Kilojoules (89 Calories); 1.6 g Total Fat (0.4 g Mono, 0.3 g Poly, 0.8 g Sat); 2 mg Cholesterol; 16 g Carbohydrate; 2 g Fibre; 3 g Protein; 143 mg Sodium

---

ABOUT WHITE BALSAMIC VINEGAR
Less sweet and more mild than regular balsamic vinegar, the white variety will not overpower other flavours. It is made from white wine vinegar and concentrated grape juice.

TIP
When making salsas or chutneys, it is wise to let the flavours sit and blend properly rather than serving them as soon as they are made. In fact, these dishes are often considered more balanced and flavourful the next day. Simply prepare, cover and leave overnight in the refrigerator.

Balsamic vinegar and pepper highlight an often-overlooked aspect of fresh strawberries – their ability to blend well with, rather than overshadow, other ingredients. Further enhanced by chèvre, this ensemble is both captivating and surprising.

Jalapeño Corn Soup

Butter	5 mL	1 tsp.
Chopped onion	125 mL	1/2 cup
Chipotle sauce (if unavailable, mix chopped jalapeño chillies with smoky barbecue sauce (see Tip, below)	7 mL	1 1/2 tsp.
Prepared vegetable stock (broth)	375 mL	1 1/2 cups
Frozen corn kernels	375 mL	1 1/2 cups
Unthickened (single) cream	60 mL	1/4 cup
Salt	0.5 mL	1/8 tsp.

Melt butter in a saucepan on medium. Add onion and jalapeño chillies and cook until onion is soft.

Add stock and corn. Simmer for about 10 minutes until corn is softened. Using a hand blender, process until smooth (see Safety Tip, page 34). Strain through a sieve, pressing solids with the back of a spoon. Discard solids.

Stir in cream and salt. Chill for about 4 hours until cold. Serves 4.

1 serving: 347 Kilojoules (83 Calories); 3.1 g Total Fat (0.8 g Mono, 0.3 g Poly, 1.6 g Sat); 8 mg Cholesterol; 13 g Carbohydrate; 2 g Fibre; 2 g Protein; 221 mg Sodium

---

GARNISH
Sprigs of fresh parsley

TIP
Store any leftover jalapeño chillies in an airtight container in the fridge.

Chilled and **velvety smooth** yet contrasted with an **intense, smoky** jalapeño chilli heat, this southwestern-influenced soup refreshes and **invigorates** all at once.

Coconut Lime Chicken Salad Cocktails

Coconut milk	125 mL	1/2 cup
Brown sugar	15 mL	1 tbsp.
Lime juice	15 mL	1 tbsp.
Dried crushed chillies	2 mL	1/2 tsp.
Seasoned salt	2 mL	1/2 tsp.
Thinly sliced cooked chicken	325 mL	1 1/3 cups
Julienned carrot (see How To, below)	125 mL	1/2 cup
Thinly sliced red capsicum (bell pepper), about 5 cm (2 inch) long slices	125 mL	1/2 cup
Rocket, lightly packed	500 mL	2 cups

Whisk first 5 ingredients together until sugar is dissolved. Add next 3 ingredients and toss. Chill, covered, for 1 to 2 hours.

Arrange rocket in 6 martini or cocktail glasses. Spoon chicken mixture over top. Serves 6.

1 serving: 519 Kilojoules (124 Calories); 7.2 g Total Fat (1.0 g Mono, 0.6 g Poly, 4.9 g Sat); 28 mg Cholesterol; 6 g Carbohydrate; 1 g Fibre; 10 g Protein; 157 mg Sodium

HOW TO JULIENNE
To julienne, cut into thin matchstick-like strips.

GARNISH
Lime peel

This **inspired** salad cocktail delivers the **flavours** of the **tropics** presented in a most **unconventional** manner. **Whimsical** in presentation but seriously **delectable** in taste.

Tapenade Toasts

Baguette bread slices, cut at a sharp angle, about 12 mm (1/2 inch) thick	4	4
Olive oil	15 mL	1 tbsp.
Soft goat (chèvre) cheese	60 mL	1/4 cup
Black olive tapenade	60 mL	1/4 cup
Chopped fresh basil	15 mL	1 tbsp.

Arrange bread slices on a baking tray. Brush with olive oil. Bake in a 175°C (350°F) oven for about 10 minutes until golden. Turn over and brush with olive oil. Bake for about 5 minutes until golden.

Spread with goat cheese and tapenade. Sprinkle with basil. Cut in half diagonally. Makes 8 toasts.

1 toast: 251 Kilojoules (60 Calories); 5.1 g Total Fat (3.1 g Mono, 0.6 g Poly, 1.1 g Sat); 2 mg Cholesterol; 3 g Carbohydrate; trace Fibre; 1 g Protein; 126 mg Sodium

---

ABOUT TAPENADE
The original tapenade hailing from Provence was a purée of capers, olives, anchovies and olive oil. The result was a salty, full-bodied spread for bread. Today, a tapenade can contain many different ingredients – you can even purchase varieties based on the specific type of olive used. It is becoming more and more common to find combinations that stray away from the olive entirely, such as artichoke and red capsicum (bell pepper) tapenades.

A diagonal cut of a baguette can present a **perfect canvas** for **simple**, expertly chosen **ingredients**. This rustic **arrangement** belies the **sophistication** of flavours.

Nut, Cheese and Fruit Bites

Mixed baby greens	250 mL	1 cup
Small fresh strawberries, stems removed	12	12
Soft goat (chèvre) cheese	75 mL	1/3 cup
Large unpeeled pear, cut into 6 mm (1/4 inch) slices	1	1
Lemon juice	15 mL	1 tbsp.
Blue cheese, crumbled	175 mL	3/4 cup
Pecans, walnuts and hazelnuts, toasted (see How To, below)	250 mL	1 cup

Arrange mixed greens on a serving tray.

Make 2 crosscuts from tip of each strawberry, almost, but not quite, through to base. Spread cuts open and fill with goat cheese. Arrange over greens.

Toss pear slices in lemon juice. Top slices with blue cheese. Arrange over greens.

Arrange nuts over fruit. Serves 6.

1 serving: 1122 Kilojoules (268 Calories); 22.7 g Total Fat (9.5 g Mono, 5.6 g Poly, 5.1 g Sat); 16 mg Cholesterol; 11 g Carbohydrate; 4 g Fibre; 8 g Protein; 224 mg Sodium

---

HOW TO TOAST NUTS
Although raw nuts are perfectly fine for snacking, toasting them brings out an aroma and depth of flavour not apparent in the raw product. To toast nuts, seeds or coconut, place them in an ungreased frying pan. Heat on medium for 3 to 5 minutes, stirring often, until golden. To bake, spread them evenly in an ungreased shallow pan. Bake in a 175°C (350°F) oven for 5 to 10 minutes, stirring or shaking often, until golden.

This **colourful** small plate is only one **example** of how you can **showcase** your own exquisite culinary style. Serve your favourite fruits, cheeses and nuts in unlimited **combinations**. Let each individual taste come together and speak in **unison**.

Salty-sweet Croustades

Walnut halves, toasted (see How To, page 208)	12	12
Honey	50 mL	3 tbsp.
Baby green leaves	12	12
Pieces of Reggiano Parmigiano cheese, about 6 mm (1/4 inch) thick, 5 cm (2 inches) long (about 43 g, 1/2 oz.)	12	12
Mini croustade shells (see Tip, below)	12	12
Balsamic vinegar	15 mL	1 tbsp.

Coat walnuts with honey.

Place 1 lettuce leaf, 1 piece of cheese and 1 walnut in each croustade shell.

Drizzle with balsamic vinegar. Makes 12 croustades.

1 croustade: 188 kilojoules *(45 Calories); 2.0 g Total Fat (0.3 g Mono, 1.0 g Poly, 0.5 g Sat); 2 mg Cholesterol; 6 g Carbohydrate; trace Fibre; 1 g Protein; 41 mg Sodium*

TIP
Croustade shells are generally found in the deli, import or biscuit sections of your local grocery store. If you have trouble finding them, you can use filo cups.

ABOUT HONEY
By varying the honey you use, you will subtly vary the flavour. Each variety is based on the type of flower the particular honeybee colony gets its nectar from. Farmers markets offer an excellent opportunity for trying different types – from blueberry to sourwood to eucalyptus. Of course, your local farmers market will sell the varieties most common to your area.

A trip to an **Italian** market is bound to **motivate** anyone who loves to cook. This recipe was **inspired** by the Italian custom of combining sharp **Parmigiano** with the honest sweetness of **honey**.

Glossary

arborio rice ~ an Italian variety of short-grain rice used for making risotto. Kernels of arborio rice are shorter and fatter than other types of short-grain rice and have a very high starch content. The starch helps to give risotto its traditionally creamy texture.

capers ~ these small flower buds are picked from bushes native to the Mediterranean and parts of Asia. They are then sun-dried and pickled in brine. Capers range in size from the very small nonpareil to stemmed caperberries, which are the size of cocktail olives. Capers should be rinsed before using to remove excess salt.

cardamom ~ native to India, this aromatic spice is a member of the ginger family. Cardamom comes in small, cranberry-sized pods. Although you can purchase cardamom already ground, for a fuller flavour it is better to use whole pods. For best results, crush the pods lightly with the back of a knife before using.

chard ~ you'll likely find several types of this beetroot relative at your greengrocer. Swiss chard will have crinkly green leaves with celery-like stalks, while ruby chard has deep green leaves with bright red stalks. You may also find rhubarb chard, which has lighter-coloured stalks and leaves. The leaves can be prepared much like spinach, while the stalks can be prepared like asparagus.

croustade shells ~ these little edible cups can be used to hold a variety of different fillings. They are made from pastry and are either baked or fried until crisp.

coconut milk ~ often used in curries, coconut milk can be quite rich and is made by combining equal parts of coconut meat and water. This mixture is simmered until foamy, then the coconut meat is strained and discarded.

coriander ~ known for both its seeds and leaves, which surprisingly taste nothing alike. The seeds are the dried ripened fruit of the plant and the leaves, also known as cilantro, are dark green and lacy. The seeds are used in baking, curries and pickling, or for beverages like mulled wines.

cumin ~ like coriander seed, cumin is a dried fruit from a plant in the parsley family. Aromatic and nutty, this spice is commonly found in curries and chilli powders.

endive ~ often confused with chicory, endive comes in three main types. Belgian endive (sometimes known as French endive, chicory or witloof) has in small cigar-shaped heads with tightly packed leaves. It is grown in darkness to prevent the leaves from turning green, which accounts for its creamy colour. Curly endive grows in loosely packed heads of lacy green leaves. Escarole has broad, slightly curved leaves that are pale green. Belgian and curly endive have a slightly bitter taste, while the flavour of escarole tends to be a bit milder.

fennel ~ with a mild licorice flavour, the celery-like stems of this plant have a sweeter and more delicate flavour than anise, another licorice-flavoured ingredient. The feathery green leaves can be eaten, but are generally used only as a garnish or for a last-minute flavour boost. Fennel seed is also used for cooking, both in savoury and sweet dishes.

garam masala ~ a mixture of as many as twelve different spices, garam masala often includes black pepper, cardamom, cinnamon, cloves, coriander, cumin, dried chillies, fennel, mace and nutmeg. This blend is said to add warmth to both the spirit and the palate, which is fitting, since the Indian word garam literally means 'warm'.

green peppercorns ~ a young, soft pepper berry, generally preserved in brine, but occasionally packed in water. Green peppercorns can also be purchased freeze-dried. Because these berries are under-ripe, they tend to have a milder flavour than other types of pepper.

hoisin sauce ~ occasionally referred to as Peking sauce, this sweet and spicy sauce is often found in Chinese cooking. Made from soybeans, garlic, chilli peppers and spices, hoisin is generally quite thick and is often used as a table condiment or to add flavour to meat dishes or stir-fries.

marjoram ~ an ancient herb, related to mint. When this ingredient is called for, sweet marjoram is what you're looking for (wild marjoram refers to oregano). The flavour is mild, sweet and somewhat similar to oregano. Another variety, pot marjoram, has a stronger and slightly bitter flavour.

mirin ~ a sweet wine, golden in colour and generally with low alcohol content. This ingredient is often used in Japanese cooking to add sweetness and flavour. Mirin is also sometimes known as rice wine.

miso ~ also known as bean paste, miso is an important ingredient in Japanese cuisine. Miso is made from fermented soy beans. The consistency is usually similar to peanut butter and is available in a variety of flavours and colours. Generally, lighter colours of miso are good for more delicately flavoured dishes, while darker colours work well with bolder flavours.

Old Bay seasoning ~ a blend of more than twelve herbs and spices, this mixture was created by a German-American immigrant named Gustav Brunn in 1939. The flavour of Old Bay seasoning is often associated with seafood, particularly crab.

olive oil ~ a flavourful and fragrant oil, often found in Mediterranean cooking. The flavour and colour can vary depending upon growing region, crop condition and the process used to press or filter the oil. Generally, the deeper the colour of the oil, the more intense the flavour. Olive oils tend to have lower smoke-points than other oils, so be careful when frying.

panini bread ~ this Italian bread is generally quite thin and is used for grilled sandwiches. Translated, panini is Italian for 'small bread'.

panko breadcrumbs ~ generally used for coating fried foods in Japanese cooking. Their coarseness helps create a perfectly crunchy crust.

pappadum ~ similar in appearance to a tortilla, this thin, wafer-like bread is made using lentil flour. You'll likely find pappadums in a variety of flavours and sizes in your grocery store or specialty food store. They can either be fried, baked or grilled over an open flame.

plantain ~ often known as a cooking banana, the plantain is a large, firm variety of banana that must be cooked before eating. The colour of a plantain's skin will tell you which stage of ripeness it's at. Green is under-ripe, yellow is ripe and black is over-ripe. Plantains are consumed at all stages of ripeness and are generally very starchy.

polenta ~ similar to porridge, this cornmeal mixture hails from northern Italy. Very versatile, polenta can be eaten as a side dish or as a breakfast item, hot with butter or cooled until firm, then cut and fried. Polenta can also be flavoured with cheeses such as Parmesan or Gorgonzola. In some delicatessens, you'll also find a firm version of polenta that can be sliced and grilled or fried.

prosciutto ~ translated from Italian, prosciutto simply means 'ham'. This type of ham is generally seasoned, salt-cured and dried. The meat is then pressed, which gives it a firm, dense texture. There are several varieties of prosciutto available, all of which are fine to eat without cooking. In fact, cooking prosciutto too much will toughen it, so it is best added at the last minute so it's just heated through.

rice paper rounds ~ these translucent papers are generally made from a mixture of water and rice flour. They come in a variety of sizes and shapes. Rice paper rounds are first rehydrated in hot water, then stuffed with fillings and served as-is or deep-fried.

salsa verde ~ generally a mixture of tomatillos, green chillies and coriander, salsa verde literally means 'green salsa'.

sesame oil ~ there are two basic types of sesame oil. The lighter is good for a variety of applications from salad dressings to frying and has a nutty flavour. The darker variety is much stronger-tasting and is often used in Asian cooking to add flavour.

shallots ~ related to onions, shallots are favoured for their milder flavour. Shallots are cooked like onions, but they more closely resemble garlic in appearance. Shallots grow bulbs with multiple cloves, each separated by a papery skin. Fresh green shallots (or spring onions) can be purchased seasonally, but red shallots are more commonly available.

suey choy ~ also known as Chinese cabbage, suey choy is cylindrical and has light green leaves. It's similar in flavour to bok choy.

tarragon ~ this aromatic herb has a flavour similar to anise and is commonly used in a variety of French dishes, including the well-known béarnaise sauce. Take care when using tarragon in your cooking, as its assertive flavour can easily overpower other ingredients.

wasabi paste ~ also known as Japanese horseradish, this green-coloured condiment has a sharp and spicy flavour. Sushi and sashimi are commonly served with both wasabi paste and soy sauce. Wasabi is made from the root of a plant related to horseradish. Some Asian markets may carry fresh wasabi, but powdered is also available.

Menu Suggestions

Sometimes matching flavours can be a tricky feat. We've taken away some of the guesswork and provided a number of menu options based on either four or six guests. Be as creative as you like and select your own groupings, or use one of the following as a guide.

For 4

Jalapeño Corn Soup, page 172
Seared Scallops Verde, page 80
Seta Antojitos Especial, page 112
Margarita Chicken Lollipops, page 60
Lavalicious Chocolate Kisses, page 152

Coconut Chilli Soup, page 42
Smoked Tuna and
Wasabi Cream in Endive Boats, page 78
Braised Hoisin Spareribs, page 166
Miso Mushroom Risotto with Scallops, page 44
Ginger-poached Pears, page 156

Seared Beef Carpaccio
with Peppercorn Mushrooms, page 50
Panini Sticks with Dipping Trio, page 32
Praline Pecans, Beetroot and Blue Cheese
on Baby Greens, page 84
Raspberry Crème Brûlèe, page 148

For 6

Dukkah Beef Skewers
with Wine Reduction, page 118
Spiced Jam with Heady
Garlic and Cambozola, page 14
Tostada Cups with Lemony
Lentils and Spinach, page 18
Herb Olive Feta Mélange
over Grilled Asparagus, page 92
Pomegranate Jellies, page 154

Butter Chicken with
Spinach and Pappadums, page 46
Walnut Ginger Crisps, page 68
Strawberry Salsa with Goat Cheese
and Melba Toast, page 170
Curried Chicken Samosa Strudel, page 100
Vanillacotta with Liqueur, page 158

Prosciutto-wrapped Bread Sticks
with Cantaloupe Purée, page 168
Tapenade Toasts, page 176
Calabrese Bites, page 164
Rocket Pesto Ravioli with
Browned Butter Pine Nuts, page 104
Sun-dried Tomato and
Leek Mussels, page 36
Cappuccino Meringue Stack, page 146

Tip Index

Avocado, pitting and slicing 72

Beetroot, roasting 84
Beetroot, cutting and peeling 84
Bones, cutting and covering 58

Cantaloupe, buying 168
Cheeses, soft, cutting 76
Chicken drumettes, Frenching 60
Chillies, removing seeds and handling 94
Chutneys, serving 170
Coconut, toasting 178
Cooked sauces, testing thickness 88

Deep frying, testing oil temperature for 106
Dough cylinders, forming 64

Eggplant (Aubergine), baking 98
Eggplant (Aubergine), salting 98
Eggs, separating and beating 68

Garlic, roasting 14
Garnishing 38

Herbs, adding 28
Hot liquids, processing safely 34

Jalapeño chillies, storing 172
Jerk seasoning, making and storing 108
Julienne, cutting 174

Marshmallows, melting 150
Mushrooms, enoki,
    purchasing 114

Mushrooms, portobello,
    removing gills of 12
Mushrooms, wild, using 16
Mussels, cooking 36

Nuts, toasting 178

Olives, pitting 92

Plantains, buying and peeling 66
Poached pears, slicing 156
Ponzu sauce, substitution 114
Potatoes, microwaving 54
Prawns (shrimp), butterflying 52
Prawns (shrimp), buying 34
Prawns (shrimp), deveining 26

Ribs, sweet-and-sour-cut, buying
    and garnishing 166
Rice paper, working with 102
Rocket, description of 104

Salsas, serving 170
Scallops, cooking 80
Searing 80
Seeds, toasting 178
Skewers, soaking 138
Squid, cooking 90

Tuna, cooking 134

Vanilla sugar, making 158

Recipe Index

Aioli Dip, Lemon 32
Almond Brie Croutons on Apple-dressed
    Spinach 76
Apple-dressed Spinach, Almond Brie
    Croutons on 76
Asparagus, Herb Olive Feta Mélange
    over Grilled 92

Bacon, Potato Crostini with Caramelised 20
Banana Boats, Crisp Cinnamon 144
Basil and Pepper Shortbread, Pine Nut, ... 64
Beef
    Dukkah Beef Skewers with Wine
        Reduction 118
    Grecian Beef Pastries 28
    Seared Beef Carpaccio with
        Peppercorn Mushrooms 50
Beetroot Coulis, Seafood with Horseradish 26
Beetroot and Blue Cheese on Baby Greens,
    Praline Pecans, ... 84
Beverages
    Blue Lagoon 8
    Bueno Beer Margaritas 8
    Canadian Snowbird 8
    Mojitos 9
    Orange Truffletini 9
    Piña Colada Martini 9
    Pomcosmo 9
Bisque, Seafood 34
Blintz Cups, Smoked Salmon 38
Blue Lagoon 8
Bok Choy, Caramel Pork Tenderloin on 94
Braised Hoisin Spareribs 166
Bread Sticks with Cantaloupe Purée,
    Prosciutto-wrapped 168
Brie Croutons on Apple-dressed Spinach,
    Almond 76
Bueno Beer Margaritas 8
Butter Chicken with Spinach and
    Pappadums 46
Butter Pine Nuts, Rocket Pesto
    Ravioli with Browned 104

Calabrese Bites 164
Canadian Snowbird 8
Candied Chicken Sticks 138
Cannellini Mousse, Parmesan Cones with 110
Cantaloupe Purée, Prosciutto-wrapped
    Bread Sticks with 168
Cappuccino Meringue Stack 146
Caramel Pork Tenderloin on Bok Choy 94
Caramel Rum S'Mores 150

Carpaccio with Peppercorn Mushrooms,
    Seared Beef 50
Cheese and Fruit Bites, Nut, ... 178
Chicken
    Butter Chicken with Spinach and
        Pappadums 46
    Candied Chicken Sticks 138
    Chicken Saltimbocca Spikes 120
    Coconut Lime Chicken Salad
        Cocktails 174
    Crispy Jerk Chicken Rolls 108
    Curried Chicken Samosa Strudel 100
    Mahogany Chicken Waves 128
    Margarita Chicken Lollipops 60
    Thai Chicken on Lemongrass Skewers 122
    Warm Ginger Chicken over Spinach 82
Chicken Saltimbocca Spikes 120
Chilli Heat, Seafood Mango Summer Rolls with
    Cool Herbs and 102
Chilli Prawns (shrimp), Peanut Noodle
    Cakes with Sweet 52
Chilli Soup, Coconut 42
Chilli Squid on Garlic Peas 90
Chilli Vegetable Skewers, Sesame 132
Chilli-crusted Medallions 130
Chips with Cocomango Dip, Fiery Plantain 66
Chive, Lemon and Poppy Seed Shortbread 64
Chocolate Kisses, Lavalicious 152
Coriander Shortbread, Pecan, Curry and 64
Cinnamon Banana Boats, Crisp 144
Coconut Chilli Soup 42
Coconut Lime Chicken Salad Cocktails 174
Coconut Scallops, Five-spiced Crepes with 22
Cod on Ginger-spiked Cucumbers,
    Miso-glazed 86
Corn Cakes with Lime Sauce, Seafood 72
Corn Soup, Jalapeño 172
Coulis, Seafood with Horseradish Beetroot 26
Crab Sushi Squares 62
Cranberry Port Jus, Walnut Pesto-crusted
    Lamb with 58
Creamy Wild Mushrooms on Pastry Points 16
Crème Brûlée, Raspberry 148
Crepes with Coconut Scallops, Five-spiced 22
Crisp Cinnamon Banana Boats 144
Crispy Jerk Chicken Rolls 108
Crostini with Caramelised Bacon, Potato 20
Croustades, Salty-sweet 180
Croutons on Apple-dressed Spinach,
    Almond Brie 76
Cucumbers, Miso-glazed Cod on
    Ginger-spiked 86

Curried Chicken Samosa Strudel	100
Curry and Coriander Shortbread, Pecan,	64
Dip, Lemon Aioli	32
Dip, Sun-dried Tomato	32
Dip, Tzatziki Herb	32
Dukkah Beef Skewers with Wine Reduction	118
Eggplant (Aubergine) Rolls, Feta and Herb	98
Endive Boats, Smoked Tuna and Wasabi Cream in	78
Feta and Herb Eggplant (Aubergine) Rolls	98
Feta Mélange over Grilled Asparagus, Herb Olive	92
Fiery Plantain Chips with Cocomango Dip	66
Figs, Halvah Ice-cream Sundaes with Orange Honey	142
Fish & Seafood	
Chilli Squid on Garlic Peas	90
Chilli-crusted Medallions	130
Crab Sushi Squares	62
Five-spiced Crepes with Coconut Scallops	22
Halibut Bites in Peppered Panko Crust	70
Leek-wrapped Ginger Scallops with Soy Glaze	124
Miso Mushroom Risotto with Scallops	44
Miso-glazed Cod on Ginger-spiked Cucumbers	86
Peanut Noodle Cakes with Sweet Chilli Seafood	52
Salmon with Herb Sabayon	88
Seafood Bisque	34
Seafood Corn Cakes with Lime Sauce	72
Seafood Mango Summer Rolls with Cool Herbs and Chilli Heat	102
Seafood with Horseradish Beetroot Coulis	26
Seared Scallops Verde	80
Smoked Salmon Blintz Cups	38
Smoked Salmon Rice Rolls	114
Smoked Tuna and Wasabi Cream in Endive Boats	78
Sun-dried Tomato and Leek Mussels	36
Tuna Skewers	134
Five-spiced Crepes with Coconut Scallops	22
Fries with Jalapeño Lime Dip, Sweet Polenta	56
Fruit Bites, Nut, Cheese and	178
Garlic and Cambozola, Spiced Jam with Heady	14
Gazpacho, Mango	40
Garlic Peas, Chilli Squid on	90
Ginger Chicken over Spinach, Warm	82
Ginger Crisps, Walnut	68
Ginger-poached Pears	156
Ginger Scallops with Soy Glaze, Leek-wrapped	124
Ginger-spiked Cucumbers, Miso-glazed Cod on	86
Goat Cheese and Melba Toast, Strawberry Salsa with	170
Goat Cheese Potato Skins, 'Uptown'	54
Grecian Beef Pastries	28
Halibut Bites in Peppered Panko Crust	70
Halvah Ice-cream Sundaes with Orange Honey Figs	142
Herb Dip, Tzatziki	32
Herb Eggplant (Aubergine) Rolls, Feta and	98
Herb Olive Feta Mélange over Grilled Asparagus	92
Herb Sabayon, Salmon with	88
Herbs and Chilli Heat, Seafood Mango Summer Rolls with Cool	102
Hoisin Spareribs, Braised	166
Honey Figs, Halvah Ice-cream Sundaes with Orange	142
Horseradish Beetroot Coulis, Seafood with	26
Ice-cream Sundaes with Orange Honey Figs, Halvah	142
Jalapeño Corn Soup	172
Jalapeño Lime Dip, Sweet Polenta Fries with	56
Jam with Heady Garlic and Cambozola, Spiced	14
Jellies, Pomegranate	154
Jerk Chicken Rolls, Crispy	108
Lamb with Cranberry Port Jus, Walnut Pesto-crusted	58
Lavalicious Chocolate Kisses	152
Leek Mussels, Sun-dried Tomato and	36
Leek-wrapped Ginger Scallops with Soy Glaze	124
Lemon Aioli Dip	32
Lemon and Poppy Seed Shortbread, Chive,	64
Lemongrass Skewers, Thai Chicken on	122
Lemon Thyme Sorbet	162
Lemony Lentils and Spinach, Tostada Cups with	18
Lentils and Spinach, Tostada Cups with Lemony	18
Lime Chicken Salad Cocktails, Coconut	174
Lime Dip, Sweet Polenta Fries with Jalapeño	56
Lime Sauce, Seafood Corn Cakes with	72
Liqueur, Vanillacotta with	158
Lollipops, Margarita Chicken	60

Mahogany Chicken Waves 128
Mango Gazpacho 40
Mango Summer Rolls with Cool Herbs and
    Chilli Heat, Seafood 102
Margarita Chicken Lollipops................................. 60
Meatballs, Rosemary-spiked............................... 126
Meatless
    Almond Brie Croutons on
        Apple-dressed Spinach 76
    Coconut Chilli Soup 42
    Creamy Wild Mushrooms on Pastry Points...... 16
    Feta and Herb Eggplant (Aubergine) Rolls.... 98
    Fiery Plantain Chips with Cocomango Dip 66
    Herb Olive Feta Mélange over
        Grilled Asparagus 92
    Jalapeño Corn Soup................................... 172
    Lemon Thyme Sorbet 162
    Mango Gazpacho 40
    Mushroom Risotto Balls............................... 106
    Nut, Cheese and Fruit Bites 178
    Panini Sticks with Dipping Trio 32
    Parmesan Cones with Cannellini
        Mousse.. 110
    Pear Puff Tart 24
    Praline Pecans, Beetroot and Blue Cheese
        on Baby Greens 84
    Rocket Pesto Ravioli with Browned Butter
        Pine Nuts 104
    Salty-sweet Croustades 180
    Savoury Shortbread Trio............................... 64
    Sesame Chilli Vegetable Skewers 132
    Seta Antojitos Especial 112
    Spiced Jam with Heady Garlic and
        Cambozola.. 14
    Strawberry Salsa with Goat Cheese
        and Melba Toast 170
    Sweet Polenta Fries with Jalapeño
        Lime Dip 56
    Tapenade Toasts....................................... 176
    Tostada Cups with Lemony Lentils
        and Spinach.. 18
    'Uptown' Goat Cheese Potato Skins................ 54
    Walnut Ginger Crisps 68
Melba Toast, Strawberry Salsa with
    Goat Cheese and 170
Meringue Stack, Cappuccino............................. 146
Miso Mushroom Risotto with Scallops.................... 44
Miso-glazed Cod on Ginger-spiked
    Cucumbers 86
Mojitos 9
Mousse, Parmesan Cones with Cannellini........... 110
Mushroom Risotto Balls 106
Mushroom Risotto with Scallops, Miso 44
Mushrooms on Pastry Points, Creamy Wild............ 16

Mushrooms, Seared Beef Carpaccio with
    Peppercorn... 50
Mussels, Sun-dried Tomato and Leek 36

Noodle Cakes with Sweet Chilli Seafood,
    Peanut.. 52
Nut, Cheese and Fruit Bites............................... 178
Nuts, Rocket Pesto Ravioli with
    Browned Butter Pine 104

Olive Feta Mélange over Grilled Asparagus,
    Herb... 92
Orange Honey Figs, Halvah Ice-cream
    Sundaes with.. 142
Orange Truffletini 9

Panini Sticks with Dipping Trio 32
Panko Crust, Halibut Bites in Peppered................. 70
Pappadums, Butter Chicken with Spinach and 46
Parmesan Cones with Cannellini Mousse 110
Pastries, Grecian Beef 28
Pastry Points, Creamy Wild Mushrooms on............. 16
Peanut Noodle Cakes with Sweet Chilli
    Seafood 52
Pear Puff Tart 24
Pears, Ginger-poached...................................... 156
Pecan, Curry and Coriander Shortbread.............. 64
Pecans, Beetroot and Blue Cheese on
    Baby Greens, Praline 84
Pepper Shortbread, Pine Nut, Basil and................ 64
Peppercorn Mushrooms, Seared Beef
    Carpaccio with 50
Peppered Panko Crust, Halibut Bites in 70
Pesto Ravioli with Browned Butter Pine Nuts,
    Rocket 104
Pesto-crusted Lamb with Cranberry
    Port Jus, Walnut 58
Piña Colada Martini 9
Pine Nuts, Rocket Pesto Ravioli
    with Browned Butter 104
Pine Nut, Basil and Pepper Shortbread 64
Plantain Chips with Cocomango Dip, Fiery 66
Polenta Fries with Jalapeño Lime Dip, Sweet 56
Pomcosmo 9
Pomegranate Jellies 154
Poppy Seed Shortbread, Chive, Lemon and........... 64
Pork
    Braised Hoisin Spareribs 166
    Calabrese Bites 164
    Caramel Pork Tenderloin on Bok Choy 94
    Chicken Saltimbocca Spikes 120
    Chilli-crusted Medallions 130
    Pork Souvlaki with Savoury Yoghurt 136
    Potato Crostini with Caramelised Bacon 20

Prosciutto-wrapped Bread Sticks
  with Cantaloupe Purée 168
Roasted Spinach Portobellos 12
Pork Souvlaki with Savoury Yoghurt 136
Pork Tenderloin on Bok Choy, Caramel 94
Port Jus, Walnut Pesto-crusted Lamb
  with Cranberry 58
Portobellos, Roasted Spinach 12
Potato Crostini with Caramelised Bacon 20
Potato Skins, 'Uptown' Goat Cheese 54
Praline Pecans, Beetroot And Blue Cheese
  on Baby Greens 84
Prosciutto-wrapped Bread Sticks with
  Cantaloupe Purée 168

Raspberry Crème Brûlée 148
Ravioli with Browned Butter Pine Nuts,
  Rocket Pesto 104
Rice Rolls, Smoked Salmon 114
Risotto Balls, Mushroom 106
Risotto with Scallops, Miso Mushroom 44
Roasted Spinach Portobellos 12
Rocket Pesto Ravioli with Browned Butter
  Pine Nuts 104
Rosemary-spiked Meatballs 126
Rum S'Mores, Caramel 150

S'Mores, Caramel Rum 150
Sabayon, Salmon with Herb 88
Salads
  Almond Brie Croutons on
    Apple-dressed Spinach 76
  Coconut Lime Chicken Salad Cocktails 174
  Praline Pecans, Beetroot and Blue Cheese
    on Baby Greens 84
  Warm Ginger Chicken over Spinach 82
Salmon Blintz Cups, Smoked 38
Salmon Rice Rolls, Smoked 114
Salmon with Herb Sabayon 88
Salsa with Goat Cheese and
  Melba Toast, Strawberry 170
Saltimbocca Spikes, Chicken 120
Salty-sweet Croustades 180
Samosa Strudel, Curried Chicken 100
Savoury Shortbread Trio 64
Savoury Yoghurt, Pork Souvlaki with 136
Scallops Verde, Seared 80
Scallops with Soy Glaze, Leek-wrapped Ginger .. 124
Scallops, Five-spiced Crepes with Coconut 22
Scallops, Miso Mushroom Risotto with 44
Seafood, see Fish & Seafood
Seared Beef Carpaccio with
  Peppercorn Mushrooms 50
Seared Scallops Verde 80
Sesame Chilli Vegetable Skewers 132

Seta Antojitos Especial 112
Shortbread Trio, Savoury 64
Shortbread, Chive, Lemon and Poppy Seed 64
Shortbread, Pecan, Curry and Coriander 64
Shortbread, Pine Nut, Basil and Pepper 64
Skewers with Wine Reduction, Dukkah Beef 118
Skewers, Sesame Chilli Vegetable 132
Skewers, Thai Chicken on Lemongrass 122
Skewers, Tuna 134
Smoked Salmon Blintz Cups 38
Smoked Salmon Rice Rolls 114
Smoked Tuna and Wasabi Cream
  in Endive Boats 78
Sorbet, Lemon Thyme 162
Soups
  Coconut Chilli Soup 42
  Jalapeño Corn Soup 172
  Mango Gazpacho 40
  Seafood Bisque 34
Souvlaki With Savoury Yoghurt, Pork 136
Soy Glaze, Leek-wrapped Ginger
  Scallops with 124
Spareribs, Braised Hoisin 166
Spiced Jam with Heady Garlic
  and Cambozola 14
Spinach and Pappadums, Butter Chicken with 46
Spinach Portobellos, Roasted 12
Spinach, Almond Brie Croutons
  on Apple-dressed 76
Spinach, Tostada Cups with Lemony Lentils and .. 18
Spinach, Warm Ginger Chicken over 82
Squid on Garlic Peas, Chilli 90
Strawberry Salsa with Goat Cheese and Melba
  Toast 170
Strudel, Curried Chicken Samosa 100
Sundaes with Orange Honey Figs,
  Halvah Ice-Cream 142
Sun-dried Tomato and Leek Mussels 35
Sun-dried Tomato Dip 32
Sushi Squares, Crab 62
Sweets
  Cappuccino Meringue Stack 146
  Caramel Rum S'Mores 150
  Crisp Cinnamon Banana Boats 144
  Ginger-poached Pears 156
  Halvah Ice-cream Sundaes with
    Orange Honey Figs 142
  Lavalicious Chocolate Kisses 152
  Pomegranate Jellies 154
  Raspberry Crème Brûlée 148
  Vanillacotta with Liqueur 158
Sweet Polenta Fries with Jalapeño Lime Dip 56

Tapenade Toasts 176
Tart, Pear Puff 24

Thai Chicken on Lemongrass Skewers 122
Thyme Sorbet, Lemon 162
Toasts, Tapenade 176
Tostada Cups with Lemony Lentils and Spinach ... 18
Tuna and Wasabi Cream in Endive Boats,
    Smoked 78
Tuna Skewers 134
Tzatziki Herb Dip 32
'Uptown' Goat Cheese Potato Skins 54

Vanillacotta with Liqueur 158
Vegetable Skewers, Sesame Chilli 132
Verde, Seared Scallops 80

Walnut Ginger Crisps 68
Walnut Pesto-crusted Lamb with Cranberry
    Port Jus 58
Warm Ginger Chicken over Spinach 82
Wasabi Cream in Endive Boats,
    Smoked Tuna and 78
Wine Reduction, Dukkah Beef Skewers with 118

Yoghurt, Pork Souvlaki with Savoury. 136

Measurement Tables

Throughout this book, measurements are given in metric and imperial measure. To compensate for differences between the two measurements due to rounding, a full metric measure is not always used. The cup used is the standard 8 fluid ounce. Temperature is given in Celsius and degrees Fahrenheit. Baking pan measurements are in centimetres and inches as well as litres and quarts. An exact metric conversion is given below as well as the working equivalent (Metric Standard Measure).

Oven Temperatures

Celsius (°C)	Fahrenheit (°C)	Celsius (°C)	Fahrenheit (°F)
80°	175°	175°	350°
95°	200°	190°	375°
110°	225°	205°	400°
120°	250°	220°	425°
140°	275°	230°	450°
150°	300°	240°	475°
160°	325°	260°	500°

Pans

Metric - Centimetres	Imperial - Inches
20 x 20 cm	8 x 8 inch
22 x 22 cm	9 x 9 inch
22 x 33 cm	9 x 13 inch
25 x 38 cm	10 x 15 inch
28 x 43 cm	11 x 17 inch
20 x 5 cm	8 x 2 inch round
22 x 5 cm	9 x 2 inch round
25 x 11 cm	10 x 4 1/2 inch tube
20 x 10 x 7.5 cm	8 x 4 x 3 inch loaf
22 x 12.5 x 7.5 cm	9 x 5 x 3 inch loaf

Spoons

Metric Standard Measure Millilitre (mL)	Metric Exact Conversion Millilitre (mL)	Imperial Measure
0.6 mL	0.5 mL	1/8 teaspoon (tsp.)
1.2 mL	1 mL	1/4 teaspoon (tsp.)
2.4 mL	2 mL	1/2 teaspoon (tsp.)
4.7 mL	5 mL	1 teaspoon (tsp.)
9.4 mL	10 mL	2 teaspoons (tsp.)
14.2 mL	15 mL	1 tablespoon (tbsp.)

Cups

Metric Exact Conversion Millilitre (mL)	Metric Standard Measure Millilitre (mL)	Imperial Measure
56.8 mL	60 mL	1/4 cup (4 tbsp.)
75.6 mL	75 mL	1/3 cup (5 1/3 tbsp.)
113.7 mL	125 mL	1/2 cup (8 tbsp.)
151.2 mL	150 mL	2/3 cup (10 2/3 tbsp.)
170.5 mL	175 mL	3/4 cup (12 tbsp.)
227.3 mL	250 mL	1 cup (16 tbsp.)
1022.9 mL	1000 mL (1 L)	4 1/2 cups

Dry Measurements

Metric Exact Conversion Grams (g)	Metric Standard Measure Grams (g)	Imperial Measure Ounces (oz.)
28.3 g	28 g	1 oz.
56.7 g	57 g	2 oz.
85.0 g	85 g	3 oz.
113.4 g	125 g	4 oz.
141.7 g	140 g	5 oz.
170.1 g	170 g	6 oz.
198.4 g	200 g	7 oz.
226.8 g	250 g	8 oz.
453.6 g	500 g	16 oz.
907.2 g	1000 g (1 kg)	32 oz.

Casseroles

Canada & Britain		United States	
Exact Metric Measure	Standard Size Casserole	Exact Metric Measure	Standard Size Casserole
1.13 L	1 qt. (5 cups)	900 mL	1 qt. (4 cups)
1.69 L	1 1/2 qts. (1 1/2 cups)	1.35 L	1 1/2 qts. (6 cups)
2.25 L	2 qts. (10 cups)	1.8 L	2 qts. (8 cups)
2.81 L	2 1/2 qts. (12 1/2 cups)	2.25 L	2 1/2 qts. (10 cups)
3.38 L	3 qts. (15 cups)	2.7 L	3 qts. (12 cups)
4.5 L	4 qts. (20 cups)	3.6 L	4 qts. (16 cups)
5.63 L	5 qts. (25 cups)	4.5 L	5 qts. (20 cups)